MULDOON

A TRUE CHICAGO GHOST STORY

TALES OF A FORGOTTEN RECTORY

ROCCO A. FACCHINI

& DANIEL J. FACCHINI

ILLUSTRATIONS BY

DAVID R. FACCHINI

4650 North Rockwell Street • Chicago, Illinois 60625

www.lakeclaremont.com

Muldoon: A True Chicago Ghost Story:
Tales of a Forgotten Rectory
by Rocco A. Facchini & Daniel J. Facchini

Published September, 2003 by:

4650 N. Rockwell St.
Chicago, IL 60625
773/583-7800; lcp@lakeclaremont.com
www.lakeclaremont.com

Publisher's Cataloging-in-Publication
(*Provided by Quality Books, Inc.*)

Facchini, Rocco A.
Muldoon : a true Chicago ghost story : tales of a forgotten rectory / by Rocco A. Facchini and Daniel J. Facchini ; illustrations by David R. Facchini.—1st ed.
p. cm.
Includes bibliographical references and index.
LCCN 2003107614
ISBN 1-893121-24-0

1. Haunted places—Illinois—Chicago. 2. Muldoon, Peter James, 1862-1927. 3. Ghosts—Illinois—Chicago. 4. Church buildings—Illinois—Chicago—Miscellanea. 5. Catholic Church. Archdiocese of Chicago (Ill.)—Miscellanea. I. Facchini, Daniel J. II. Title.

BF1473.M85F33 2003 133.1'2977311
QBI03-200474

Printed in the United States of America by United Graphics, an employee-owned company based in Mattoon, Illinois.

08 07 06 05 04 10 9 8 7 6 5 4 3 2

to two positive influences in my life–

my wife, Della, and

Reverend William A. Schumacher.

PUBLISHER'S CREDITS

Cover design by Timothy Kocher. Interior design and layout by Charisse Antonopoulos. Illustrations by David Facchini. Editing by Laura Gabler. Proofreading by Sharon Woodhouse, Daniel Facchini, and Karen Formanski. Index by Karen Formanski.

TYPOGRAPHY

The text of *Muldoon* was set in Walbaum Roman and Verdana, with headers in Walbaum Italic.

Table of Contents

Foreword

VIRTUALLY EVERY WEDNESDAY at 12:30 P.M., a motley group of aged men gather at Gulliver's Restaurant on Howard Street, which marks the border between Chicago and Evanston. They chose Gulliver's because its menu is the size of an old Missale Romanum and the restaurant smells like a church basement after a potluck supper. Its ceiling is covered with a marvelous collection of antique light fixtures, and although the group rarely drinks, one can always wet one's whistle to celebrate an event—usually survival from surgery or remission of one or another form of cancer.

Gulliver's is the kind of place where curates used to gather with their classmates on their day off, which, coincidentally, was usually a Wednesday. It's the kind of place where priests once gathered to exchange gossip, always more abundant than grace. Over portions that are heart attacks on a plate, they could gripe about having to do three funerals while their pastors got the weddings, or they might parse the latest chancery bulletin reminding them to change from black fedoras to Panama hats three days after the Feast of the Ascension.

Since the close of Vatican II in 1965, dramatic changes in the culture of the clergy have altered the way priests interact. But these men, most of whom are resigned priests, still continue to gather and talk as if they had just been ordained. Now they talk about their kids and their grandchildren. They talk about religion, politics, and the issues of the day. They are men educated at the level of lawyers or physicians but interact like police officers or firefighters. There are more than 46,000 priests in the United States, and during lunch at Gulliver's, one learns that they all know each other. They reminisce about the good old days, when harmless drugstore remedies such as mineral oil and milk of magnesia prescribed by their mothers and by the sister infirmarian at the seminary did the trick. Today their ailments are far more serious. There are clogged arteries and malignant colons, diabetes and failed kidneys. They are on the back nine, waiting for God. They look back with faith, forward with hope, and at one another with charity.

Most were diocesan priests, but there is the occasional Jesuit, Passionist, or Dominican. The majority of these men were ordained more than 40 years ago, before the start of Vatican II. They began their priestly careers saying Mass in Latin with their behinds to the people. Within a decade, most were presiding in English and facing the faithful. Like their hero from Vatican II, Pope John XXIII, they opened the windows of their minds to admit fresh air, which eventually blew many of them out of their ministries.

They call themselves the Romeos—an acronym standing for Retired Old Men Eating Out—a title given them by Carole, who is the wife of Marty Hegarty, one of the originators of the group. The Romeos have no bylaws, dues, or minutes. Members just show up. As the group grows, Gulliver's just adds another table. The regulars like it that way. Most of them have a healthy disrespect for authority, viewing it as nonproductive. They welcome anyone, including still active priests and a rare bishop, as well as priests who resigned under a cloud.

All are active Catholics. The vast majority are solidly married. (The divorce rate among resigned and married priests is only about 4 percent.) None became rich men, but all did well in spite of the fact that they got a late start and had to work later in life to accumulate a nest egg that would permit them to live comfortably while they waited for God.

For most of these men, the train has made its last stop. But the weekly clinical recitation is healthy. The exercise is therapeutic. They can empty out their heads and souls while they fill their bellies. There's Jim Wilbur, who, after being a priest for 14 years, went on to be the editor of hymnals and the original Missalette and is the group's grammarian and walking encyclopedia. Barry Rankin was a probation officer after having served as a Passionist priest for 16 years and was one of the founders of the Catholic Theological Union at the University of Chicago. Bob McClory served in several Chicago parishes before resigning and becoming a writer; he is currently a journalism professor at Northwestern University. There are also Frank McGrath, Dominic Cronin, Bill McGlynn, Ed Gilpatric, and a cast of others who come whenever they can. Then there is Rocco, a lovable guy who at one time was one of the rarities among the predominantly Irish or German priests in Chicago—an Italian. Rocco always has great stories to contribute, from recalling anecdotes from his 15 years of ministry to cracking a morbid joke about his failing health condition. As the oldest son of immigrant parents and a native Chicagoan himself, Rocco always brings a unique perspective to the table conversation, like having actually attended Our Lady of the Angels grammar school before it burned down in 1958.

And then he has his Muldoon stories. A few years ago Father Tom Millea wanted to hear some of these popular ghost stories firsthand and asked Rocco to share. Rock's stories are told with enthusiasm and in the context of the Catholic Church in Chicago. Eventually, Jerry Maloney, a former assistant at Saint Charles Borromeo after Rocco's time, had his own stories to tell as well, building upon the legend of Muldoon. In a culmination of discussing his story, listening to others, and researching scattered articles on the life of Bishop Muldoon, it's taken Rocco almost 40 years to write all of it down.

This fascinating book is larded with stories and characters. It is a biography of an institution that is filled with faults because it is filled with people. It explores the life and times of Bishop Peter Muldoon and recollects the many stories of his ghost that priests have spread by word of mouth for years. Rocco has written it with loving scholarship. One cannot make this book up. As a novel, no publisher would ever touch it. Today, as the Archdiocese of Chicago silently benefits from the work and planning of Muldoon, there are still priests alive, active or resigned, who will swear on their indelible marks on the ghost stories of this bishop. Though not a resigned priest, I've heard all of these stories time and again over linguini at Gulliver's. It's all true.

Honest.

—Tim Unsworth, *National Catholic Reporter*

MULDOON

A TRUE CHICAGO GHOST STORY

∞

TALES OF A FORGOTTEN RECTORY

The Right Reverend Peter J. Muldoon, D.D. (Reprinted from *Silver Jubilee: Saint Charles Borromeo: 1885–1910.*)

Lifting the Veil

EVERY YEAR, JUST BEFORE Halloween, the local Chicago talk shows and newspapers are full of ghost stories in the Windy City. There's the story of Resurrection Mary, a young blonde woman adorned in flowing white who suddenly appears and vanishes in the traffic in front of Resurrection Cemetery on Archer Avenue. There is also the ghostly legend of the two drowned altar boys who, in 1871, warned parishioners of Holy Family Church about the impending Great Chicago Fire. In neighboring Evanston, you will hear of the ghost that, in the darkness of night, rises soaking from cold Lake Michigan and paces outside the locked east gate of Calvary Cemetery. There are volumes of books on hauntings and ghost stories from the Chicago area, not to mention the rest of Illinois, the remaining United States, and all over the world. There are ghost stories from China, Canada, the Caribbean Islands, England, Ireland, Wales, Scotland, France, Italy, and, of course, Transylvania—yet among them all, I have never found the story of Muldoon.

October 31, 1999—Halloween. My younger son, David, stopped by with his roommates to rummage through the house for last-minute costumes. His friends, Greg and Mike, sat with me in the family room while my boy plundered the closets and basement. Then David yelled to me from afar, urging me to tell my Muldoon stories. Ever since my boys were small, I have regaled them with the ghost stories of Peter J. Muldoon, a Chicago Catholic priest, the founding bishop of the Diocese of Rockford, Illinois, and builder of Saint Charles Borromeo Church on the Near Southwest Side of Chicago. At the time of construction, the church was located at the northwest corner of 12th and Cypress Streets. In 1909 the street names were changed to what are now Roosevelt Road and Hoyne Avenue, respectively. After his death on October 8, 1927, it was said that Muldoon haunted the rectory and church of Saint Charles Borromeo until it was slated for demolition by wrecking ball in 1968 and leveled thereafter.

My Muldoon stories are not tall tales. Most of them come from my personal paranormal experiences while I served as a newly ordained Roman Catholic priest at Saint Charles from 1956 to 1960. Some of them are secondhand from others who surrounded me in the parish during that time. Usually, their experiences only confirmed the happenings that I, too, could not logically explain.

To my surprise, Greg and Mike had already heard some of these stories from David. I later found that, through the years, both of my sons had repeated these stories in school, at campfires, in pubs. With great enthusiasm, my son and his friends suggested that I chronicle these stories. From that day forward, I vigorously pondered the idea of writing a book about the ghost of Muldoon.

But write a book? Writing a book is not a simple matter for a 70-year-old man in my physical condition. During the last 12 years, I have had two quadruple bypasses, have had a series of angiograms and angioplasties, and have lost kidney function. Due to these factors, I am subjected to kidney dialysis three times a week, am on a strict diet, and have restricted water and fluid intake. I am almost always physically and mentally fatigued. Because my debilitating condition knocks the starch out of me, I find that I have only fragments of time in which I am able to focus my thoughts and capture my experiences. On the contrary—to me, writing a book is an overwhelming and difficult task, indeed.

I have personal reservations as well. For the most part, I am a quiet person and like to keep my personal matters private. Up to now I have enjoyed years of anonymity, especially after enduring the somewhat-celebrity status of a diocesan priest for 15 years prior to living the life of a layperson. I went from Our Lady of the Angels grammar school, to Quigley Preparatory Seminary, to Saint Mary of the Lake Seminary, to assignments at the Chicago parishes of Saint Charles Borromeo, Saint John Bosco, and Our Lady, Help of Christians. I remember the religious life I once lived—which, until now, I had always chosen to keep as an unspoken past. To write about Muldoon means describing my religious life and the lives of the people with whom I lived at Saint Charles Borromeo. I would have to reconstruct and rekindle that distant past and unveil it.

And I have never before tried to write a book! Never in my wildest imagination had I even thought of it. The prospect of getting enough words out on a printed page is daunting to me. I am not a good typist, my computer skills are nil, and I don't know if I can muster enough words to captivate a reader. Nor have I ever before felt the urgency to write a book. Until now.

Virtually every priest who once served at Saint Charles Borromeo is now deceased. Who else is left then to tell the strange and engaging stories about the life of Bishop Peter J. Muldoon and the legend of his ghost? So, despite my challenges and personal reservations, the idea of revisiting my days at Saint Charles Borromeo—the good, the bad, the unexplainable—compels me to put pen to paper.

I believe the story I am about to tell. I lived it. To the best of my knowledge, it has not yet been publicly revealed. Ever since that Halloween, the legend of Muldoon has resonated in my mind, and as the days go on, my need to tell it grows stronger. My intent is not to present a scientific, historical, or theological study. This book will not be strictly a biography or an autobiography, nor is it an analysis of the Catholic priesthood. What you are about to read is a series of engaging stories that resurrect my life as a Catholic priest at Saint Charles Borromeo, explain the impact of Bishop Muldoon in the Catholic Church and at this parish, and detail the bizarre range of events that related primarily to me, Father Bill Schumacher, Father Ray Goedert, and Pastor Kane (whose name I have changed).

In 1956 I walked into Saint Charles Borromeo newly ordained with the consecrated oils fresh on my palms—eager, idealistic, and totally unprepared for the difficult years ahead of me. With this first appointment I had to grow up quickly on the mean streets of Chicago's most vile slums, awed and chastened by the sheer depth of human misery around me. My equilibrium and strength during those hard times came from desperate prayer, coupled with the affirming and spiritual conversations with Father Schumacher and Father Goedert. And living among us was a presence that we came to believe was the ghost of Bishop Muldoon. Four years later, I left sobered, fatigued, and indelibly altered with the seed of resigning from ministry planted deep inside of me.

Chapter One

The Haunted Rectory

AT THE CORNER OF RUSH AND Chestnut Streets, just a block away from the historic Chicago Water Tower and the bustle of Michigan Avenue, stands Quigley Preparatory Seminary, a Catholic entry-level school of theology for teenage boys aspiring to the diocesan priesthood. (The word *seminary* is derived from the Latin noun *semen*: a seed carefully sown into an environment of strong faith, to develop strong and vigorous stock.) Today, the old school seems like a lost homeless person among the modern glistening skyscrapers—unkempt, injured, and misplaced. Much has changed since I was a student there, when the religious compound comprised some of the largest structures in the area. The Gothic court buildings of the seminary stood tall and majestic then—a beacon amid a sea of shabby houses, scattered parks, and cheap taverns. In particular, I remember a balmy spring afternoon in 1949, just weeks away from my graduation ceremony at Holy Name

Cathedral. This was the first time I had ever heard of a haunted rectory in a Chicago parish.

At the time I attended Quigley, the minor seminary of the Archdiocese of Chicago was a five-year school, offering three years of high school and two years of college preparation. Quigley was different from most minor seminaries in the nation because students did not have to move away from home to attend. Most other seminaries were boarding schools in which students were isolated from family life and society. But Quigley was founded on the progressive idea that a minor seminarian could pursue studies leading to the priesthood while living a typical life with his family. The devout purpose of the school was to support the young seminarian in his growth as a person of prayer, spirituality, and intellectual understanding, as a trained messenger who would bring the Good News of Jesus Christ to the waiting world. Classes were held five days a week, with Thursdays off and classes on Saturday. This kept fellows from common adolescent social activities, especially dating. The school days were from 9:00 A.M. to 3:15 P.M. daily, with a guaranteed three hours of homework each night.

Classes had a strong emphasis on language studies. Everyone studied English along with a modern language tied to his ethnic background, such as Italian, Polish, Lithuanian, or German. The predominantly Irish student body learned French. Latin was required through all five years, and classic Greek with its ancient alphabet was required of all seminarians from sophomore year onward. Quigley's difficult and complex curriculum was weighted heavily in the humanities, reflecting a wide range of thoughts and feelings of every human age and providing deep insight into the human psyche. Each student studied a significant amount of literature, including Latin classics such as Caesar's *Gallic Wars* and works by Cicero as well as Greek literature pieces like Xenophon's *Anabasis* and

Quigley Preparatory Seminary, before the addition of the west wing on Rush Street. (Reprinted from *Diamond Jubilee of the Archdiocese of Chicago, 1920.*)

Oedipus Rex by Sophocles. Ancient, medieval, and modern history was studied. English literature concentrated on the works of Shakespeare: *Julius Caesar, The Merchant of Venice,* and *Hamlet.* The significance of all these classical studies was to develop a well-rounded parish priest as someone able to understand, connect with, and counsel desperate souls.

My senior English literature professor was Father Vincent Casey, a monotonous and no-nonsense teacher. He had a round, serious face and stood about six feet tall, weighing some 200 pounds. He was meticulous, from his trimmed, graying black hair at his temples, to his pristine black cassock, to his well-organized teaching style—he always stuck to his appointed text. Though his lectures were lethargic and dull, Father Casey was a teacher who, in order to perform, needed total control over his pupils. When the class faded from his attention, the easily flustered Father Casey would nervously start coughing and stuttering, his face would turn crimson, and he would begin rapidly distributing demerits. Like so many other mild men of the cloth, when Father Casey blew his stack, it was catastrophic and everyone ran for cover.

On this particular spring afternoon in 1949, Father Casey was concentrating on the main characters of Shakespearean plays. According to him, each of the Bard's characters was a worthwhile study of human behavior. As we discussed the significance of Banquo's ghost from *Macbeth,* Father Casey made a rare interruption from the coursework that I never forgot. He paused for a moment and completely changed the subject. With uncommon energy, he began talking about an old rectory in the archdiocese—a dark, musty place that smelled like death and had a creaky staircase leading to the second floor. Soberly, he told the class about the ghost of a former pastor who had been seen walking up the staircase, almost bumping into a priest from the house. Father Casey went on to tell of this ghost who made itself known many times, year after year, both visually and sonically. The story seemed fresh to him, as if it had just happened recently. And Father Casey told it very seriously. When some of the class chuckled in disbelief, he deliberately cleared his throat and retold his story, speaking in a stronger and more nervous tone. This was something that obviously shook him up. I could tell that he wanted to be heard. He wanted to be believed.

Father Casey gave few details or facts that would reveal the name or location of the haunted rectory. He just kept saying it was a dark, ominous place. After discussing it briefly, he turned back to the lecture topic just as abruptly as he had

The Haunted Rectory. (Illustration by David Facchini.)

begun telling the ghost story. It was apparent Father Casey was uncomfortable speaking of ghosts and spirits. Though he never brought up his ghost story again, and I can't remember ever discussing the story with any of my classmates, I was enthralled by his short narration. I could not help but wonder where that haunted rectory could be.

∞

Having been a priest, I can appreciate Father Casey's need to cut his ghost story short. Priests know that the discussion of the spirit world is dangerous territory, as it can easily challenge traditional Catholic beliefs. Historically and to this day, the Catholic Church refuses to officially recognize the concept of ghosts. Though Christianity promises immortality through the spiritual afterlife of heaven and hell, it rejects the concept of the manifestations of spirits returning to earth. Therefore, there is a vague, yet significant, difference between the definition of a human soul and a ghost: The soul goes to a completely different conscious afterlife unknown to our physical world, while a ghost, seen as a tortured spirit trapped in our material world, for unexplainable reasons does not move on to future rest. For men of the cloth, it might be all right to joke superficially or to allude briefly to ghostly happenings. However, it is more comfortable to blanket unexplained occurrences with silence, avoid deep theological debate, and move on to safer topics.

Chapter Two

A Call from God

MY CALLING TO THE PRIESTHOOD began long before I attended Quigley. My mother felt this was to be my destiny ever since I was a little boy of five. It was my first day of kindergarten at the Ryerson Public School on Ridgeway Avenue, a block south of Chicago Avenue. Education was important to my parents, since their formal education in Italy had extended only to the third grade. As the first-born of poor immigrants, I understood that my role was to be the spokesman for the family. They wanted me, as spokesman, to get a good education so that I could fully understand American culture and figure out how our family fit into it. But I couldn't speak any English because Italian was the language spoken exclusively at home.

On my first day of kindergarten, after I had been enrolled and positioned in class for about an hour, I quietly left the classroom, walked down the long corridor, and left the school. I ambled one block north to Chicago Avenue, already a busy thoroughfare at that time. I was very small yet somehow managed to negotiate myself across the vast street busy with streetcars, trucks, pushcarts, and peddlers and found my way home to a locked front door. At the same time, my mother, Maria, came to pick me up from school only to find I wasn't there. Frantically, she, the teachers, and even the principal searched for me. I was nowhere to be found. Trusting her maternal instincts, my mother raced back to our first-floor apartment, where she found me lumped into a heap and sobbing at the door. She was frantic and relieved, and in the fine, time-honored Italian way, she whacked me across the face with her left hand. I can still feel the sting of her wedding ring. Slapping me and hugging me at the same time, she shouted in Italian, *Dove sei stato? I tuoi maestre e Io abbiamo cercato in vano. Mi hai fatto impazzire.* "Where have you been? Your teachers and I have been searching for you! You've made me half crazy."

Red-eyed and quivering, I blurted, *Vorrei entrare alla scuola Cattolica.* "I want to go to Catholic school!"

Taken aback by my response, she cried, *Questo è il tuo destino. Tu sarai sacerdote.* "This is your destiny! You shall be a priest." That's how my journey to the priesthood began.

A Catholic education was a hard sell to my shoemaker father, Gerardo. Catholic school was expensive, at a dollar a month for tuition, while public school was free. Additionally, the nearest parish was predominantly Irish, and I would be one of the first Italian students to attend Our Lady of the Angels. Beyond all of this, my father was deeply anticlerical. He was born in a Papal State in Italy and had the deepest disdain for his former landlord, the Church. People of the early 1900s did not forget that Pope Pius IX, himself an Italian, fought furiously against Italy's unification, sending French and Austrian mercenaries to slaughter his own people. It was a clerical atrocity that recognized Pius IX as *Il Carneface* (the Hangman Pope). (Only after the reunification of Italy led by Garibaldi in 1870 did hanging cease in the Papal States.) As result, the Pope and his church lost the trust and love of his blood brothers, never to be fully regained . . . even to this day.

Despite my father's protests, he listened to my mother's desires. In our Italian family, Pa ruled the roost for the entire world to see, but behind closed doors, Ma ran the show. Submitting to her friendly persuasion, he decided that as the oldest son, I would be the first to enter the local parochial school.

My calling to the priesthood deepened through the example of marvelous men at Our Lady of the Angels parish, like Monsignor Joe Cussen, Father Joe Curielli, and Father Len Mattei. I admired these priests with a respect that was common at that time. I looked to men like Father Tom Long, Father Ray Naughton, and Father Jim Quinn as role models for my future religious life. What I admired and remember most about them all collectively is that they all would stand out in front of church after Masses on Sunday morning with the hundreds of parishioners and involve themselves in various conversations of friendship and community.

After graduation from Our Lady of the Angels, I enrolled in an incoming freshman class of 286 at Quigley Preparatory Seminary. To be accepted into Quigley, the student required a letter of recommendation from his pastor expressing his judgment that the new applicant was entering the school with the purpose of becoming a priest. The boy had "the call from God."

I remember my daily ride to Quigley on the packed Chicago Avenue streetcar at 7:30 A.M. Fare with a student pass was four cents. On many a Saturday morning, conductors would refuse student passes, doubting that any high school conducted Saturday classes. I boarded at Lawndale Avenue, and as the big red streetcar clanged its way east, I noted the distance by streets—Central Park, Kedzie, Western, Damen, Ashland, Halsted, over the Chicago River, past Montgomery Ward, LaSalle Street, State Street, Wabash Avenue, to my final destination, Rush Street. When I found a seat, I reviewed Latin vocabularies or worked my way through Greek conjugations. All the while, I passed through the then Italian, Ukrainian, and Polish neighborhoods, whizzing past churches like Holy Rosary, the Ukrainian Cathedral of Saint Nicholas, Holy Innocents, Saint Boniface, Saint John Cantius, the Moody Bible Institute, and Holy Name Cathedral.

Five years later, filled with all kinds of knowledge and basic spiritual principles like obedience to God and love for mankind, I graduated from Quigley Preparatory Seminary with the class of 1949. The once large freshman class of 286 had dwindled to 82 graduates who, with their families and friends, filled Holy Name Cathedral for Mass and to receive our gold graduation crosses from Samuel Cardinal Stritch.

From Quigley, it was on to Saint Mary of the Lake Seminary in Mundelein for seven years of education in philosophy and theology. The pontifical seminary was known as "the Rock," given that it was a tough place in which to exist. The studies were vigorous, with some classes taught in Latin. Strict obedience to the rules reigned over all activities. It was run much like a strict monastery. We entered school in early September and stayed until May, with no home visits except for two weeks between semesters in January. During the first three summers, students of philosophy generally had summer assignments, such as teaching catechism at poor parishes or being counselors at Maryville Academy and Angel Guardian Orphanage. Then, as theologians, we spent our final three summers at the seminary villa in Clearwater Lake, Wisconsin. Thanksgiving and Christmas were spent at the seminary. Parents were allowed a two-hour visit in designated classrooms during the three visiting Sundays each semester. They could leave two pounds of food.

The Great Silence prevailed over the dorms, where each seminarian had his own room. Seminarians were not allowed to speak in the residential buildings. Speaking to your neighbor as you passed in the hall or any common areas was prohibited. No one was allowed in another's room. No one was allowed a newspaper, magazine, radio, television, or phonograph and certainly not a telephone. A violation of these rules could lead to expulsion. The only time we could read newspapers or magazines was on Christmas Day, and even then the disciplinarian censored these materials, cutting out worldly articles and photographs. To us, the tough training was the obstacle course for ordination—it was the price to pay.

On the day before my ordination, Samuel Cardinal Stritch interviewed each of the 30 candidates individually. The rector had provided him with a file card on each man to be ordained. The cardinal knew that my mother had come from Agnone, high in the Abruzzi Mountains of Italy, and that my father had come from Sora di Frosinone, a small city not far from Rome. The cardinal encouraged me to visit Agnone, famous for the fabrication of church bells, fine Italian jewelry, and metalwork. He went on to assure me that I would be sent to a community with a large Italian constituency. This pleased me. I was going to be one of the few Italian priests in the archdiocese. Al Corbo and I were the only Italians in our class, and at the time, there were only about 20 priests of Italian heritage in Chicago—a minuscule population compared to the Irish, Polish, and German priests. In fact, all through seminary training, I felt I was a novelty because much was always made of my being Italian. There were many parishes with hundreds of Italian families,

The ordination of the Class of 1956 in the main chapel of St. Mary of the Lake Seminary, Mundelein, Illinois. (From the Facchini family collection.)

much like the growing Italian community in my home parish of Our Lady of the Angels. Would I get the chance to work in an Italian community?

The prevailing joke about being appointed for the first time was that the cardinal had a huge dartboard in the chancery, marked with the locations of all the Chicago parishes. Supposedly taking a dart with the name of a newly ordained priest attached to it, the cardinal, with a flip of his wrist, would determine the priest's destiny for the years to come. So, where would I be sent?

Tuesday, May 1, 1956, was the first time the Feast of Saint Joseph the Worker was celebrated in the universal Church. I was proud to be one of the 30 ordained for the Archdiocese of Chicago that day. My parents, other family members, and friends all attended. It was a glorious day. My First Solemn High Mass took place on Sunday, May 6, 1956, in my home parish of Our Lady of the Angels. At the request of the pastor, I stayed at the rectory that night. I had made it! My destiny had been fulfilled.

After the celebrations at home, I returned with my classmates to the seminary for the "Ad Auds" (*ad confessiones audiendas*), an oral exam on moral principles before seminary faculty members—a litmus test for hearing confessions. During the exam, the moral theology professors took us through the commandments with special emphasis on sexuality—the sixth commandment. They were testing for the first time our ability to discern and to make practical, moral judgments. Following the "Ad Auds," each of the newly ordained was allowed time at home before receiving his first letter of appointment. This letter from the Archdiocesan Chancery Office arrived at my parents' home in late June of 1956 with the starting date of July 7. I was assigned to Saint Charles Borromeo at Roosevelt Road and Hoyne Avenue.

∞

On the impoverished Near West Side of Chicago, the pastor at Saint Charles Borromeo parish asked for an Italian-speaking assistant although the once dense Italian population of the neighborhood had dwindled significantly. At that time, the archdiocese viewed Italian priests to be in low demand in Chicago, and they were not readily accepted in every parish. Knowing that Italian priests were undervalued, Pastor Kane felt confident that his request could easily be filled as in prior years. Years after my time at Saint Charles Borromeo, I learned through the Italian League of Priests that an Italian priest would be accepted at a parish only at the request of the pastor. Among the predominantly Irish pastors, this request was rare.

Chapter Three

Failed Expectations

ABOUT A WEEK BEFORE MY FIRST official day at Saint Charles Borromeo, I found myself full of excitement and on a 45-minute trolley bus ride to meet my first pastor. (The Chicago Avenue streetcar line was abandoned on May 11, 1952.) After years of studying and anticipation, I was finally ready to apply my skills in an actual parish. At last, I was an ordained parish priest and now had the opportunity to live God's ministry. This was a special day for me, so I dressed formally, wearing my new black suit, shiny leather shoes, crisp Roman collar, and Panama hat. On the ride, I briefly wondered to myself why it took a series of phone calls to finally get in touch with the pastor and why he insisted on meeting me outside of the rectory. But I dismissed his initial quirkiness and instead envisioned a warm fraternal welcome from my priestly brother.

Alighting from the middle doors of the bus at Roosevelt Road and Damen Avenue, I stepped onto crumbled concrete sidewalks. (The Damen Avenue streetcar line was abandoned on May 13, 1952.) Everything around me looked downtrodden and dilapidated: abandoned buildings, half-leveled structures waiting patiently to be demolished, vacant lots sprouting abused refrigerators, stained mattresses, blown-out tires, and other randomly strewn debris. As I looked down what was formerly 12th Street, I saw empty three-flats and vacant storefronts with shattered windows. The terrain resembled a bombed-out war zone. Clearly, this neighborhood was a slum; it had hit rock bottom with a resounding thud and showed no sign of recovery.

As planned, Pastor Kane met me on the sidewalk alongside the rectory. He and his dog, Duke, were waiting for me on Hoyne, both framed by the massive stone three-story rectory and out-of-place Gothic church of Saint Charles Borromeo in the background. Kane was dressed in disheveled and dirty sport clothes that matched the rusty color of his dog. He was wrinkled and scruffy, almost as if he had slept in these clothes for days. His pockmarked complexion and bulbous red nose almost drew attention away from his meek stature and protruding stomach. When I approached him, Kane offered me no common signs of greeting or friendship. There was no light chitchat or warm welcome. When I introduced myself and extended a handshake in friendship, he even overlooked the gesture. By now, I felt that I had forced him into this meeting. After an uncomfortable moment, he turned away from me and said, "Let's get going."

Kane led me on his short agenda, though without showing me the church, rectory, school, or convent. Our first stop was the boiler room of the decaying parish complex. Of all things, he showed me the old oil burner and the procedure to follow should the heating plant break down during winter. These seemed to be strange instructions for my first day, a hot summer afternoon. What was this all about?

After my boiler room briefing, we headed for the second and final stop of that day's orientation tour. This time, we moved into the vast bingo hall in the basement beneath the main church. The trapped air was thick with the body odor of the large bingo crowd from the day before, infused with cigarette smoke and the smell of acrid popcorn oil. He told me the hall held some 800 bingo players at dozens of oblong, green-topped tables; some players would even play 25 to 30 cards at a time. Obviously, bingo was big here, and Pastor Kane took pride in that.

Three janitors, all in their late 60s, were doing their after-Tuesday-night cleanup. They were slothlike in picking up discarded popcorn boxes, jar game tickets, and cigarette butts and in moving the dirt around rather than giving the basement a thorough cleaning. They didn't even open a window. Without ventilation, that stagnant brew of repugnant smells was encased by tight stone walls for next Tuesday's bingo crowd. As he futilely sloshed the concrete floor with a

Reverend Rocco A. Facchini, May 1, 1956. (From the Facchini family collection.)

dirty mop and dirty water, the janitor in charge approached us and introduced himself as John Uher. John then pulled Pastor Kane aside, and they got into a heated shouting match. At a distance, I couldn't hear what the argument was about. But it was clear there was deep animosity between the two of them. I stood silently off to the side during their argument while Duke barked loudly in support of his master. Pastor Kane then walked away with the gleam on his face of having won the shouting match. With the end of his argument came the conclusion of my brief orientation. He walked to the door and excused himself, saying he expected me on July 7. He had obviously had enough polite niceties.

As I walked out of the basement, I ran into one of the two exiting assistants, Father Leo. I had met Father Leo before but was unaware that he was stationed at Saint Charles. He was leaving the parish that day and was lugging boxes of books to the trunk of his car. After I said hello and offered my assistance, Father Leo was effusive in welcoming me and invited me to his room on the rectory's second floor. Within minutes, I received the brotherly welcome I had expected. He sat me down, offered me a cold soft drink from his own small personal refrigerator, and gave me some sound advice about this particular rectory and parish.

"Rocco, I am leaving here with a heavy heart. I came here a year ago already knowing that there were problems with this parish and the community. But I followed the will of the cardinal, trying to do the best that I could. I'm afraid I haven't been able to make much progress here. You will have your work cut out for you."

As a daunted look must have waned over my face, Father Leo tried to reassure me. "I don't mean to discourage you. I am sure you will do a fine job. But nothing much ever develops here. I think the glory days of Saint Charles are long gone. The people around here are disheartened, and they don't come to the church for hope and safety as they once did. There is little spirituality left in the parish."

"How have things gotten this bad?" I asked. "Why is it like this?"

"You will find out soon enough, I guess," he replied. "Just be careful of Kane. He's a man who's lost his faith. He has lost his sense of mission in preaching God's word to the poor and takes little interest in life outside the rectory walls. He sees this parish as a garbage dump filled with the people that society doesn't want: the poor, the addicts, the drunks, and the hookers. He could care less about the large black population south of Roosevelt. And he almost refuses to involve himself in the growing hospital ministry on the north end of the parish. Kane just doesn't like this parish. He's not a happy man."

Father Leo continued. "Let me give you some advice. The new fellow assistant will be Father Gaughn. Stick close to him. Kane loves to cause trouble. He will try to turn you against each other and will bad-mouth you behind each other's backs. And be careful of Irma, the housekeeper and pastor's secretary. She involves herself in everything, and if you complain to him about her, Kane will back her up. They're as thick as thieves, and she calls the shots."

Father Leo then paused with a deep breath before going on. "There are many problems here, and some very strange things happen late at night that I just can't explain."

"What do you mean?"

"I guess you will see what I mean after you finally live here for a while. I don't want to worry you unnecessarily. Maybe you will be more successful here than I was. I hope you are."

I sat quietly next to the window on my bus ride back home. I was in a reflective mood. There was so much to think about. All that I had experienced over the last few hours filled me with apprehension. This was not what I had hoped for. Inwardly, I felt the ominous clouds of Saint Charles now blocking my bright future. Could I survive this place? My assignment was open-ended without a closing date. Would I be able to last?

∞

Time would prove that Pastor Kane not only isolated himself from the harsh reality of the streets but also avoided comfortable contact with the priests who lived in the house. He seemed to live in an impenetrable bubble, avoiding the unpleasantness of the outside and instead directing himself to things inside the rectory walls that were most precious to him, like his housekeeper, his dog, his cut-glass collection, and Tuesday night bingo.

In hindsight, I think that the tour of the boiler room was meant to keep me from meeting anyone else on my initial visit. It was almost ironic that the first thing Kane showed me at Saint Charles was the boiler room. Except for the rectory that was always warm, Kane always kept the rest of the complex cold to save money. The nuns complained of the uncomfortable lack of heat in the convent and in the grammar school. The vast church was cold most of the time during frigid months; rarely did it get any heat. To me, there was nothing more jarring than celebrating early morning Mass in a cold church and holding a frozen metal chalice to my lips to see clouds of breath freezing before my eyes and frost on my eyeglasses. I later found out that one of the elderly janitors, Loveless Craig, was instructed by Kane to bang on the old steam pipes with his metal hammer during Mass, giving the sparse congregation the impression that heat was on its way. But the heat never came. In all my four years in the parish, there was never a need for emergency repair of the heating system.

Chapter Four

The Perfect Setting

MY FIRST MEETING WITH PASTOR Kane had left me a bit leery of him. His unorthodox behavior, along with Father Leo's advice, positioned me to be cautious. But prior to moving into the rectory, I resolved to hold off any further judgment and instead give him the benefit of the doubt. The rector of the major seminary, Monsignor Malachy P. Foley, had drummed this concept into us. "Look to the good side of people and to the best side of things." I resolved to look to the good side of Father Kane.

I arrived at the Saint Charles rectory on July 7, 1956, not by public transportation nor in a car of my own (I was not allowed to own an automobile at the rectory), but in my brother Jerry's battered tan Chevy. His car was quite fitting for the neighborhood. Prior to my ordination, Monsignor George Casey, vicar general of the archdiocese (and brother of my teacher at Quigley, Father Vincent Casey) had come to the seminary to explain the regulations that applied to my graduating class. By archdiocesan mandate, the newly ordained could not own a car or drink alcoholic beverages for the first five years, and we could not appear hatless in public. On the street, we were required to wear a Panama or straw hat from June 1 to Labor Day and a black fedora for the rest of the year. Because of my spartan seminary training, I didn't have much to move into the rectory. I didn't have any furniture. I only had a few personal possessions: my clothing, a tabletop radio, some books, two black cassocks, a biretta, and a new gold-plated chalice. Jerry helped me move my things in; it didn't take long.

Standing on the porch of the rectory's rear entrance, we were overpowered by the bold appearance of the fortresslike structure that stood three stories high and was capped by ornamental peaks. Father Patrick D. Gill founded the parish in 1885, and in 1891 he constructed the imposing rectory on a vast open prairie. It was the first rectory in Chicago to have a shower. At that time, the large facility was used for priest retreats and clergy meetings.

The rectory itself looked dark and Victorian, almost like a spooky Charles Adams cartoon. Its worn elegance, both inside and outside, spoke of bygone days. Walking through the door felt like suddenly stepping back into the early 1900s. It was apparent that the rectory's original lavishness had not been properly maintained. Necessary repairs had been delayed for years—perhaps in the current spirit of poverty in the neighborhood. The exterior Indiana pink limestone was stained brown from pollution and grime. Inside, the once opulent carpets were frayed and dusty, and the walls were cracked from the shifting foundation. Even the air within the building smelled old and stale.

The first floor of the rectory, designed to be its working center, was trimmed with oak paneling from the floor to the height of four feet. The two front offices on either side of the front entryway were used as meeting rooms for all kinds of

The Haunted Rectory of St. Charles Borromeo Parish. (Illustration by David Facchini.)

human services. A foyer separated the front offices from the rest of the rectory by a heavy oak door, the top half of which was made of decorative etched and frosted glass. The rest of the main floor contained a dining room, a well-lit and orderly kitchen, and a working office crowded with metal filing cabinets, parish mailing lists, frayed old books of baptismal and marriage records, and two large worn wooden office desks. Except for the bright fluorescents in the working office and the kitchen on the first floor, the house lights were ornate wall sconces and dated ceiling fixtures that gave off a dim amber glow.

The lavish dining room, worthy of a bishop, was paneled in dark cherry wood from floor to ceiling, except for mirrored panels between the floor and wall-mounted cabinets.

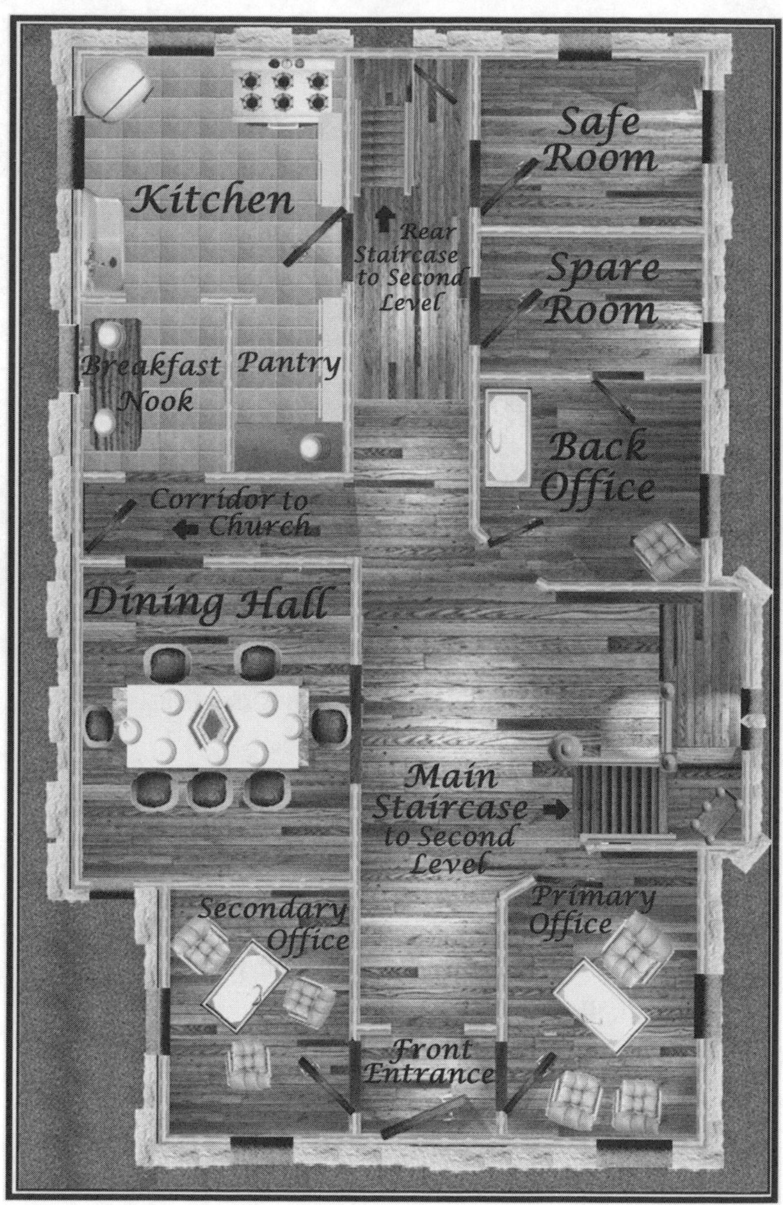

St. Charles Borromeo Rectory Floor Plan— First Floor. (Illustration by David Facchini.)

The dining room had rich maroon carpets, high-backed maroon chairs, and maroon drapes at the sole window and around the wide dining room entry. Centered from the ceiling was an impressive crystal chandelier that hung delicately over a gleaming, wooden dining room table that could seat eight comfortably. In the mirrored opening, Pastor Kane proudly displayed his elaborate cut-glass collection for all to see.

Across from the dining room was a dramatic stairway that led to the second and third floors, with a landing between each floor. The exquisite ornamental wood staining of the first floor extended up the stairway and gleamed through the carpets worn at the edge of each stair. A huge stained-glass window at the landing between the first and second floor filled the stairway with brilliant color, especially in the early morning when it harnessed the eastern sun's strong and continuous rays of light. A handsome grandfather clock stood guard at the corner of the landing, faithfully chiming every quarter hour—all day, all night. After a while, I learned to tune out its regular tolling.

All the priests assigned to the rectory lived on the second floor. My suite of rooms consisted of a bedroom and a sitting room separated by a closet and a washstand, all on the Hoyne Avenue side of the rectory. Across the hall from my room was Father's Gaughn's large sitting room, which led to his diminutive bedroom, and positioned unceremoniously on a stand in the hallway was the single community phone shared by the assistants. Being on the inside of the house, Gaughn's quarters had only two small windows; because of the usual darkness, he left his lights on most of the time. The pastor's suite was the width of the building and faced Roosevelt Road. It had a toilet, a private phone, and abundant natural light. At the back of the rectory directly across from my sitting room was a single vacant room for a resident priest. Lastly, there was one full bathroom with that famous first rectory shower for the priests of the house.

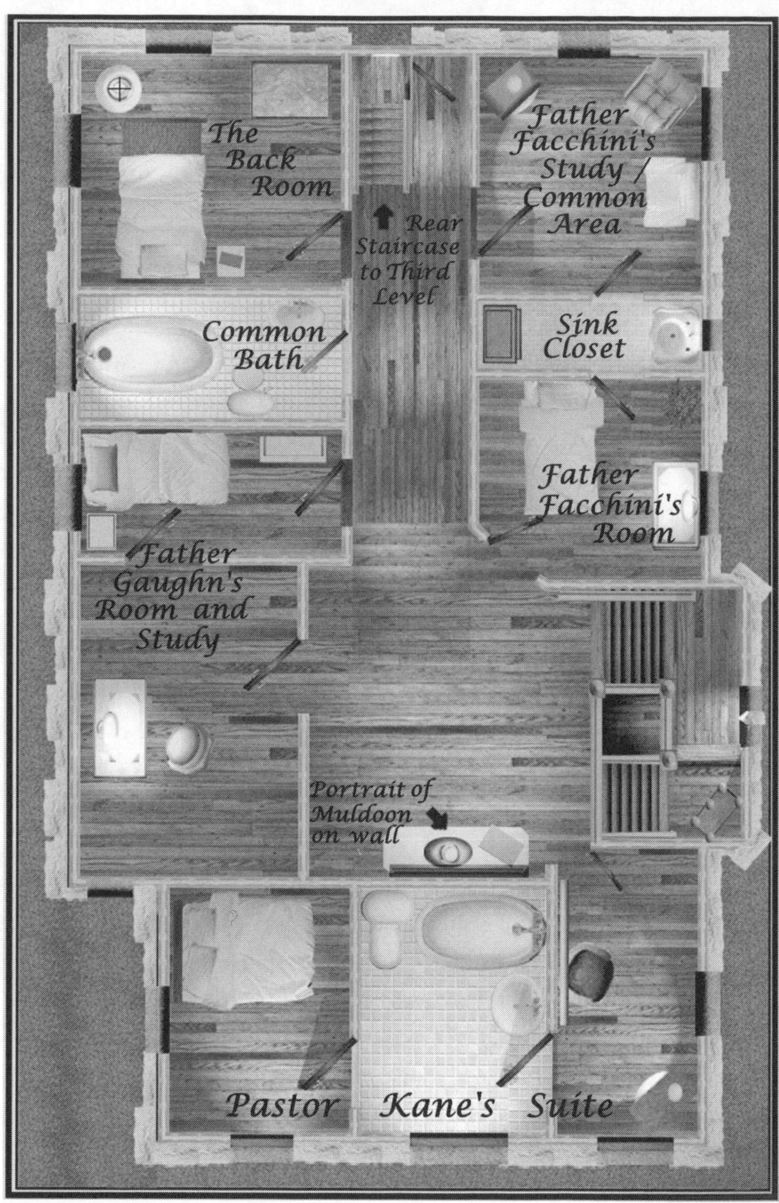

St. Charles Borromeo Rectory Floor Plan—Second Floor. (Illustration by David Facchini.)

The third floor had rooms reserved for the housekeeper, the cook, and a visiting priest. Another half dozen rooms, all locked, were crammed with relics of another age: old clothes, vestments, furniture, books, documents, pictures, and paintings.

Supporting the entire rectory was the raised concrete and stone basement that contained several different rooms. Sometime over the years, it must have flooded and was never properly dried. This resulted in a wavy and splintered hardwood floor and the pungent smell of mildew. The basement was always cold in the winter. One room in the basement stored a mimeograph machine used to grind out the weekly parish bulletin—*The Borromean*. There was another larger, vacant room that Father Schumacher would eventually use to store supplies for the Saint Vincent DePaul Society, which served the poor of the parish and the greater impoverished neighborhood. There were old clothes, used shoes, and cans of food stored here for the many beggars from Madison Street and beyond who regularly found their way to our front door. The largest room was designated for the League of Saint Anne. It was packed with boxes of cheap plastic rosaries, dashboard statues of Jesus, and Saint Anne holy water fonts. From here, Pastor Kane and Irma, the housekeeper, regularly mailed Mass cards and religious trinkets to thousands of people nationally in exchange for donations to support perpetual prayer at "The National Shrine of Saint Anne at Saint Charles Borromeo." This room was usually locked and off-limits to everyone but Pastor Kane and Irma.

Jerry helped me unpack and get settled into my new quarters, then he left for class at Loyola Law School. After seeing my brother off, I decided to introduce myself to the rectory staff. I first met Margaret, the cook, who was in the kitchen preparing a roasted leg of lamb for supper. Margaret was tiny, standing about five feet tall, and hunched over with a humped back. Her head made little movement and seemed almost buried in her shoulders. She was in her mid-50s, had a pale complexion framed by strawberry hair, and had pleasing blue eyes. Her thick Irish brogue signaled to me that she was one of the vast network of female Irish immigrants who had turned to the archdiocese seeking work as a housekeeper or cook in any one of its numerous rectories. She was very cordial and inviting, and in her, I felt that I had found an instant friend.

Margaret and I spoke for a while. Through our pleasant conversation, I learned that Father Gaughn, the other new assistant, who I had not yet met, had moved in the day before. The last time she saw him was minutes earlier, when he was going in the side entrance of the church. I then decided to visit the church, the great building of the worn parish complex that I had missed on my orientation with Kane.

I left the rectory through the side door that brought me into a covered passageway connected to the east side of the church. From the doorway, I spotted Gaughn in the front pew on his knees, deep in prayer, immersed in the soft quiet and immense beauty of the ancient church. The main altar of brilliant white marble that seemed of another world was engulfed by the rich spectrum of colors streaming softly from the sunstruck stained-glass windows. Centered on the main altar and drowning in lavish color was the golden tabernacle, flanked on each side by three golden altar candlesticks, each the height of a four-foot altar boy and faced with a brilliant silver angel at least two feet in height. Father Gaughn's solemn demeanor kept me from introducing myself. He had the reputation of being a thoughtful man of uncompromising high ideals, and I did not want to break his concentration while he prayed in this peaceful scene.

Deciding that I would wait to meet Father Gaughn at supper, I reentered the rectory. While passing the rectory's main working office on my way to the second floor, I spotted the parish housekeeper and secretary, Irma, sitting at her desk. I knocked on the open door and introduced myself. She kept our conversation hurried and brief. "Well, you must be the new one. I'm Irma, and I am very busy right now, so I don't have time to talk. I suppose Pastor Kane will let you know how things work around here soon enough. You probably have a lot of settling in to do, anyway. I will tell the pastor that you stopped by. Good day."

Irma was plain and thin. Her clipped and gruff demeanor matched her mannish looks. She wore no makeup, had an unflattering short haircut, and was dressed in simple, unadorned clothes. Irma worked in the main office daily from 9 A.M. to 3 P.M. A student from nearby Saint Mary's High School filled in from 3 P.M. to 9 P.M. As it appeared we had nothing else to say to each other, I returned to my room to await supper.

I arrived at the extravagant dining room just before 6:00 P.M. Kane was already sitting comfortably in his ornate captain's chair at the head of the long oak table, his dog lying on the Oriental rug behind him. Gaughn was sitting at his right-hand side; I sat down to Kane's left. The other five chairs at the table were empty. This was the extent of the rectory staff: the pastor, two assistants, a housekeeper, a cook, and Duke, the best fed in the house.

Parish business was conducted during mealtime. In those days in the diocese, there was no such thing as a regular staff meeting in most rectories, so the affairs of the parish were usually discussed at the dinner table. That evening, supper began with some small talk. In his naturally soft and reflective manner, Father Gaughn spoke about his life prior to coming to Saint Charles. We each talked a bit about our respective backgrounds. Then the pastor took over the conversation and got down to it.

"What is the most important day of the week?"

As Father Gaughn and I gazed at each other with puzzled looks, I presumptuously replied, "Sunday, of course."

"Quite wrong, young man," Father Kane sharply retorted. "Sunday is just a distant second. In this parish, the most important day of the week is Tuesday. Tuesday night is bingo night, and bingo is the lifeline of this parish. Nothing else is more important than bingo night. Is that understood?"

Proceeds from bingo were the most significant source of income for the parish. Every Tuesday, players would load up on buses and come from as far away as Milwaukee to play bingo at Saint Charles Borromeo; the people in our parish were too poor to play. Kane was clear that absolutely nothing could interfere with our commitment and dedication to bingo night. No prior obligations. No other pressing parish business. No family affairs. No wakes. No funerals. There was simply no excuse to be absent from Tuesday night bingo.

Kane continued in detail about our bingo responsibilities. My first duty on Tuesdays, to begin at 11 A.M., was to set out thousands of bingo cards of various colors, each with its own jackpot. The gold cards were purchased for a dollar and carried the main jackpot for the evening, $1,000. Then at 4 P.M., after an early supper, I had to be in the cashier's cage. At the entrance of the bingo hall, I would be seated behind a thick window of bulletproof glass to collect the entrance fee of a dollar. The pastor required that I wear my black cassock and that I make small conversation with the bingo players as they entered—a simple and personal inducement to keep them coming back. As the clock moved toward 7 P.M., Father Gaughn, dressed in a black suit and Roman collar, would enter my booth in the company of two male parishioners to pick up the cash at hand. We called him the "bag man," as he had to carry the sack of heavily guarded money through the hall to a private location in the rectory where it would be counted. If we had at least 800 bingo players, it would be a good night, and the parish would profit $1,000 for the evening. When the crowd was extra large, the basement of the school would be opened to make another $200 on the evening.

After collecting the cover charge, I would return to the breakfast nook in the rectory with four other volunteer money counters—usually former parishioners who returned to help the struggling parish. We were to keep a running tab on all the money that had been collected during the evening. The process would end at 10 P.M. with final results posted and revealed to all the bingo volunteers. The nights we reached our goal of $1,000 in profits, everyone cheered.

While I was responsible for the correct tabulation and record of the bingo receipts, Father Gaughn would run the jar game in a large display booth in the bingo hall. It contained all sorts of prizes: toasters, coffeepots, gaudy plaster statues, and Kewpie dolls. In addition to picking up the cash receipts from the cashier's cage, Father Gaughn would serve as a roving goodwill host, roaming the hall throughout the night to quell any possible disturbances.

As I listened to Kane discuss our bingo duties at length, I eventually interrupted. "What about our other duties?"

"Other duties?" Kane replied in instant exasperation.

"Yes. Surely there is more to Saint Charles than just bingo."

"There might be, but there is nothing more important! Gentlemen, I am a practical man—a businessman. I have run this place for the past four years, and I know what I have to do to keep our doors open. We are the tail's end of the diocese. Do you think that Cardinal Stritch gives a rat's ass about this parish? Do you really think that Mayor Daley is sitting in City Hall worried about the people in this neighborhood? Saint Charles doesn't count; this neighborhood doesn't count; these people don't count! The both of you are here because I need help keeping this place above water. I am not a spiritual priest or a dreamer. Sure, we'll say Mass and hear confessions, but I will leave most of that pious stuff to you younger guys. And, Rocco, since you are so interested, you can work in the school, manage the altar boys, work with the teens and the Legion of Mary. How does that suit you?"

Kane was cold and sarcastic as he spoke. He talked only of material things and did not speak about how to evangelize people with the Word of God. And so far, it seemed there was a lot of evangelizing needed in this neighborhood. With stars in my eyes, I wanted to proclaim the Gospel and not get caught up in the material costs that were involved. Kane and I obviously belonged to different schools of thought, and the estrangement between us was obvious. But Pastor Kane was the boss. Under my ordination vows, I was held to strict obedience to him. I was the rookie with a lot to learn and experience. I had no choice but to obey and respect him. Tough stuff.

After supper, I decided that I needed some fresh air to help collect my thoughts. So, in the heat of an urban summer evening, I decided to explore the gritty neighborhood that engulfed Saint Charles Church. The territory of the parish was divided into three distinct sections. The southern half of the parish, known as the Valley, was home to about 24,000 poor blacks, Hispanics, and Eastern Europeans. The vast, yet densely packed region stretched from Roosevelt Road to the factories and railroad tracks south of 14th Street and extended from Ashland on the east to Rockwell on the west. Unofficially, we knew most of the hovels in the Valley were infested, lacking adequate sanitary toilet facilities and running water. In the summer, the homes were hotboxes; in the winter, walk-in freezers. The northern half of the parish comprised two separate sections. The east side boasted the upcoming hospital district between Damen Avenue and Ashland Avenue that was beginning to be better served by Holy Trinity parish. The western section was between Damen Avenue and the railroad tracks past Western Avenue where many European, mainly Italian, immigrants lived and preferred the neighboring Saint Callistus parish.

A white priest strolling down the street in a Roman collar seemed to excite quite a response from the clusters of people loitering on street corners and sitting on their front porches. People naturally knew that I was from the big church on Roosevelt and Hoyne, but they seemed more surprised to see a priest just walking down the street. As I wandered through the battered neighborhood, it was obvious that something was missing. There was nothing beautiful or pleasing anywhere in sight: no grass or flowers, no parks or ball fields, no restaurants or shops or theaters—only streets and alleys strewn with garbage. The single grocery store for the area, on Roosevelt east of Oakley Avenue, sold food in unusually small quantities—two eggs, a single banana, one can of beans—for well above regular market prices. All the uplifting things that help build a healthy and responsive community were missing.

As I walked down Roosevelt, I stopped to speak to a thin black man about a foot taller than me and dressed in dirty and tattered rags with the look of being third or fourth hand-me-downs.

"Hey . . . you belong to that big church down the street?"

"Yes. My name is Father Rocco."

"Father Rocco—that's I-talian, right?"

"That's right."

"You're a tough guy then. One time I went into an I-talian neighborhood and got whooped real good. I'll be sure not to mess with you." He extended his hand. "I'm Curba Mason."

"Curba—that's an interesting name".

"Well, sir, I've never met anyone named Rocco before neither."

"Fair enough," I chuckled. "You know, Saint Charles is just down the street and our door is always open. You and your family are welcome there anytime."

"I don't think so, Father. God and I don't get along too much. He stopped listening to me a long time ago, so I quit praying. We got no business with each other now."

"Don't say that, Curba. That's not true. God is listening. He loves you!"

"Now, that's a lie! I'm supposed to believe that God loves me? If He loves me so much, how come He's never helped me in no way? He don't pay my rent. He don't pay the heat. He don't put clothes on my kids' backs. He don't put shoes on my feet, and He don't put food on my table. Now, I know you gotta tell me God loves me and such, 'cause that's your job. But God never helped me no matter how hard I asked, so I quit believin' a long time ago. He don't give a damn about us people in the Valley. God's a nothin' to me now."

I was bothered as I listened to the pain behind his grievances and was overwhelmed with how difficult it was to find a spark of faith in this parish. But how could I argue with this man? The misery of Curba's life was overpowering. He was indigent and knew there was no way out for him. He was bitter about it, too, and I can't say that I blamed him. This neighborhood was an unfortunate place where the desperately poor learned to distrust and be cynical. And here I was, a white, naive, and pious Catholic priest selling canned rhetoric about God's love. I was not deep enough in my faith to reach him. After Curba vented for about 15 minutes, his agitation seemed to soften, maybe because somebody had just taken the time to listen to him. As we parted company, I invited him to visit me at the rectory or church anytime. I never saw him again.

Later that evening, I lay awake in bed staring at the cracked ceiling in my dark room. I was humbled from the day's events. All of the problems set before me seemed insurmountable. Pastor Kane was disinterested in advancing the basic spirituality of the parish, and with him, the people of the neighborhood had weakened in their faith. The seminary did not prepare me for problems of this magnitude. I was just shoved into this foreign environment without any practical training. The seminary trained priests to be scholars and gentlemen who lived a comfortable lifestyle with three square meals a day while drawing a modest salary. We tried to understand the helplessness of poverty, in theory. We were not forced or compelled to live the hard life of the impoverished. Our comfortable cultural training made us incapable of knowing the desperation and hopelessness that chronic poverty brings.

As I thought and prayed that night, I eventually found comfort and strength in the Incarnation—that God sent his Son into the world, to become man, in order to understand all about humankind. Christ was sent here for a good reason. It made me realize that I must have been sent to Saint Charles for a good reason, too. Perhaps living among the poor was my calling. Maybe I was here to learn and understand the problems and trials the poor face every day, and to provide them with hope and consolation. Putting the idea of serving a primarily Italian apostolate on hold, I decided to make the people of the Saint Charles community my people. Through them, I hoped to become a better priest. I resolved to serve them as best I could.

∞

A rectory is an interesting hybrid facility that serves as both home and workplace for the diocesan priest. Most often, it is attached to a church and functions as the nerve center from which all parish activity flows. The parish usually takes its form and direction from the pastor's leadership. It is the pastor's strengths, beliefs, and personality that give bearing to the activity of the parish. At Saint Charles, it was apparent that Pastor Kane was incapable of elevating the life of the rectory and the surrounding slums. He was incapable of even attempting it.

During the forthcoming weeks, I would learn all about the problems that Father Leo had warned me of. If Pastor Kane did not happen to like you on any given day, he'd give you the silent treatment and ignore you as if you did not even exist. Irma monitored our phone calls by eavesdropping on the office extension, and she snooped around our rooms under the guise of "housekeeping." Dinner was usually a grim affair. Pastor Kane was often glum and silent unless we were discussing bingo. There were no seconds at supper. Leftovers were usually cut up and fed to Duke or were put away immediately after dinner was served. Eventually, Pastor Kane put a padlock on the refrigerator to keep anyone from any snacking.

The living situation with Kane was far from being brotherly. It was far from even being civil. The first assignment is critical to the development of anyone pursuing a religious life: priests, nuns, brothers, and so forth. Generally, two out of three priests who leave active ministry had disastrous first assignments. In the late 1960s, it was estimated that once the seed of clerical resignation is planted, it takes approximately five years for a priest to finalize that decision. In recent years, that time of pondering has been shortened considerably. Consequentially, there is much more forethought in first appointments. Today, the newly ordained are usually sent to good parishes with stable pastors to provide a solid head start into the ministry. The local Church has been adept at correcting the human errors of the past.

Chapter Five

This Must Be It!

IT WAS A HOT, STIFLING MID-August Saturday night five weeks into my first priestly assignment, deep in the urban slums of Saint Charles Borromeo parish. It was 8 P.M. on confession night, and I had an hour left in my unventilated confessional along the east wall of the church. As I waited for someone to receive the Sacrament of Reconciliation, my discomfort was intensified by the heavy black cassock that smothered my perspiration-soaked T-shirt. I had already spent hours of isolation in the dark and confining stall, praying for someone to serve, listening for any sign of life in the vast church: a voice, echoing footsteps, the squeak of a door. Yet I heard nothing. I was tired and needed a break.

The resonance of my movement and footsteps filled the vacant nave as I left the confessional and walked through the Gothic church to the front steps. Looking to the western horizon, the setting sun stood motionless, like a huge blood orange in the crimson sky, lacquering tenement tops in glowing auburn. The heat of the day had sapped me of my energy, and the lack of Catholics remaining in this community had deflated my spirit.

The once large Catholic population of Saint Charles had dwindled due to the massive sociological change within the parish confines. Other churches were better serving the European population at the north end of our parish. This left Saint Charles with the Valley, where there were very few Catholics to begin with. Consequently, the sacramental life—which is essential to the vitality of any Catholic church—was almost nonexistent. Very few baptisms, weddings, or funerals took place here. Anointing of the Sick was rarely requested, and confession, apparently, was not popular either. Even the celebration of Sunday Mass was commonly under-attended. Outside of the celebrant, the organist (Charles Citro), and an occasional altar boy, only a handful of regulars were in attendance. This usual emptiness of the church was intensified by its grand design, constructed to seat 1,300 parishioners comfortably. At one time, I am sure the church was crowded to capacity, but those glory days of the parish seemed long gone.

By now, I had adjusted to the fact that our basic obligation was to tend the rectory's front door to serve an endless stream of the poor clamoring for job referrals, temporary housing, or any kind of food and clothing. In that mix usually came derelicts from Madison Street begging for 25 cents for a pint of cheap wine. In effect, Saint Charles was now an urban mission located in perhaps the most affluent Catholic archdiocese in the world. The destitution of this parish could rank with the poorest pockets of Africa, India, or South America, where the beaten, uneducated, and impoverished were fated to subsist. The Valley was a wretched place to live. People here were born without opportunities and had been demeaned by life. Their spirits had been calcified by the rigidity of their environment, and they were heavily burdened with racism, unfairness, and desperation. Saint Charles, the largest structure in the neighborhood, with a proud cross atop its spire, was a towering beacon that attracted the indigent in search of a handout. As priests, we were drawn into the neighborhood's fight against poverty, ignorance, and human degradation. We had become the untrained social workers to the unwanted.

A zealous pastor driven by Christ's mission would have been able to identify the limitless opportunities available within the parish of Saint Charles. Perhaps Saint Charles could have also served the growing medical district on the parish's north end or focused upon preaching God's Word to the hopeless poor in the Valley. But Pastor Kane had shut off the possibility of serving a large black apostolate, and his personal history of exclusion had put a stop to any involvement in the emerging hospital ministry. He chose not to reach out but rather to ignore the obvious needs of the community. As far as Kane was concerned, Saint Charles was going to remain unprogressive and maintain its old-fashioned, Irish tradition of management—very routine. He must have seen himself as the anointed guardian of an unchanging past.

At 9 P.M. on this hot August night, after confession, it was my additional task as usual to shut down the entire church. Knowing the desperation of the area, we were constantly anxious that someone would desecrate the sanctity of the church during the night. I was responsible for checking and locking each exterior door of the grand old edifice each night to make sure it would be secure until morning. My routine was a careful walk-through of the entire building, first down the long side aisles, then up the wide center aisle, checking between each and every pew and searching under the seats to be sure no one had found a hiding place during the evening. Then I thoroughly checked the altar boys' sacristy, the priests' sacristy, and the baptistery. After my slow and careful inspection, I turned off the few overhead lights that had been burning. I was enveloped in total darkness except for the flickering of the sanctuary lamp, a large candle always kept burning to indicate Christ's constant presence in the tabernacle. The loving flicker of that flame in the vast darkness gave me great comfort. By the time I exited the venerable old church, it was about 9:30 P.M. All was quiet and secure.

The rectory was equally silent. Usually there was some activity in the rectory during the evening. This particular day had been so unbearably hot that each of the parish staff retreated to his or her room early, seeking comfort from an electric fan or small window air conditioner. The rectory had been shut down for the night. A small kitchen night-light dappled globs of brightness on cabinets, walls, and the shiny waxed kitchen floor. I double-checked the front and back doors of the rectory, then headed upstairs to my room.

Because we lived in such a dangerous neighborhood, it was common practice for each resident in the rectory to lock the door of his or her room from the inside with a skeleton key when going to bed. It was also part of this rectory's culture. People kept to themselves for the most part. It was not an open community.

As I came up the stairs, I noticed that Father Gaughn's door was open; he was sitting in front of a table fan, rustling through the *Chicago Tribune*. A parishioner hand-delivered a copy of the Sunday *Trib* late each Saturday night. Pastor Kane's door was closed. As usual, Kane quietly secluded himself in his suite with his loyal mutt. Margaret, Irma, and a visiting priest had also retired to their rooms on the third floor for the night. After hanging up my damp cassock to dry, changing my wet T-shirt, and refreshing myself with some cool tap water, I sank into my old, moth-eaten easy chair for a bit of TV before calling it a night. Father Gaughn came into my large sitting room and made some small talk. I was barely paying attention to him until he began to go into a tirade about the dysfunctional rectory life at Saint Charles.

"Rocco, what is going on here?"

"What do you mean?'

Father Gaughn began speaking in a loud voice with unaccustomed animation. I had never before seen him so angry. "Kane is wasting our time—I'm a priest, damn it! I'm not here to be a pit boss in a bingo hall or to be a social worker to the Madison Street drunks."

"Shhhh. Keep it down," I said, closing the door of my sitting room for a bit more privacy. "Let's not wake the entire rectory."

"Don't worry, they're all locked away in their rooms, hiding from the reality of this place. God forbid that someone notice that things aren't right in this parish! God forbid that someone say something about it! And in the meantime, we go through the motions every day. We say Mass to nobody and wait in empty confessionals. It's pointless. There are so many people out there that we could really help, and we don't. We can't because Kane won't let us. He has discouraged and stopped any idea I've had for reaching out to the people of this parish. It's so damn frustrating!"

Father Gaughn's disgust for his assignment at Saint Charles became a familiar theme that I heard time and again during our days together. Father Gaughn blasted Kane for his lack of commitment to the blacks, the poor, the Latinos, the emerging hospital ministry. He knocked Kane for his complete lack of mission, his mismanagement, and his measured distance from the priests of the house. Kane was full of it; in public, he snowballed the parishioners and bingo players, telling people of the great things taking place in the parish—but he never delivered. He just didn't care.

"And what about Irma?"

"I guess she is not very pleasant," I responded.

"Not very pleasant? The flu is more pleasant than Irma. And she has Kane wrapped around her little finger. Kane listens to her more than he listens to us! Something is not right between them. Don't you wonder why there have been over a dozen different assistant priests here over the past three years? Did you ever ask yourself why Irma has so much control?" Father Gaughn's tongue stumbled as he blurted out his words; his mouth couldn't keep up with his thoughts. "Don't be a fool, Rock. I have served in other parishes before, and I've had my fair share of bad rectory experiences, but this is beyond belief! This place is as sick as its secrets. Can't you see what's going on?"

"Hey! I'm the rookie here! I don't know what to expect from my first assignment. What am I supposed to do about Kane? What do you want from me?"

Father Gaughn had expressed many troubling and valid dilemmas that I had already seen and understood but kept to myself. Deep down, I could tell that something was wrong, with Kane's lack of mission, his zealous attitude toward making money, and his close relationship with Irma. It was enough to give a canon lawyer the shakes. Gaughn was bothered by all of this and needed to vent. I guess I had never said anything to anybody because I just didn't know what to do. Now I realized that we both felt helpless.

"The chancery needs to find out about what's going on. I don't know about you, but I am not going to stand for it. I've just got to get out of here."

Father Gaughn eventually ran out of steam, and his intensity and volume dropped down to a coarse whisper. I excused myself and Gaughn returned to his room. Once again, the rectory was quiet. Tired from the heat of the day,

I was ready for a good night's sleep to brace myself for a hot, stuffy church and an anticipated crowd of about 10 to 15 at the earliest Mass the next morning.

Suddenly without warning, a loud and thunderous explosion shattered the stillness. I heard what sounded like a locomotive crashing through the first-floor kitchen. The building shook violently, as if the entire rectory had been lifted off its foundation and dropped with a big bang. The walls moved and quivered, the furniture moved. Lights flickered off and then on again.

Needless to say, I was jolted wide-awake. I went into the hall, where I met Father Gaughn, who was also stunned. We looked at each other in silent confusion, too shocked to speak. Was it a prowler? We had no means of defending ourselves—but the noise had been too loud to have been caused by just one person. Had someone driven into the rectory? But the sound had come from the downstairs kitchen, which was not exposed to Hoyne or Roosevelt, so that did not make any sense. Why had the lights flickered on? Was it all a dream? But we were both still awake. And anyway, how could we both dream the same thing?

Then, for a split second, came a new torrent of sounds, like the rip of kitchen cabinets from plaster walls and the shattering of many window panes, like dishes, glasses, cups, silverware, pots, pans, and cooking utensils being hurled against the walls and crashing to the floor. We both heard the racket and ran down the rear stairway taking two and three steps at a time.

My heart was pounding with excitement as we arrived at the open kitchen door, expecting to find an intruder and absolute chaos. But the sounds had stopped, as if someone had suddenly turned off the flowing noise from a giant spigot. Entering the kitchen, we were astounded. Everything was quiet and in absolute order, just as it had been left by Margaret after Saturday night's supper and as I had seen it only an hour before. There was nothing broken anywhere.

What happened here? We both heard it. How could it be explained?

Silence had once again enveloped the rectory. Father Gaughn and I were thoroughly mystified. What in God's name was that volcanic explosion that shook the joists of the rectory? And what was that noise that we both heard just moments ago? Had we after all fallen asleep and shared a dream? Was it a mutual delusion? Were we both going nutty at the same time?

The sounds we both heard were memorable, lasting only brief seconds that seemed like several long minutes. They were unlike anything I had ever heard before or since.

Being men trained to logic, Father Gaughn and I quietly assembled ourselves and began looking for the source of the evening's disturbances. Together, we both searched the basement, the entire first floor, and the outside perimeter of the rectory for any signs of disruption. I walked into the hot night, down Roosevelt Road in front of the church and rectory, and then north on Hoyne to Taylor Street, looking for a collision of two vehicles that could have slammed into each other, causing such reverberation. But there was nothing. When I returned to the rectory, Gaughn told me that he had come up empty as well.

Puzzled by many unanswered questions, we gave the rectory another careful look and returned to my sitting room, saying very little. We were at a loss for words. We briefly talked about what we had heard and experienced, and coming up with no solid answers, we decided to go to bed. Perhaps we would find some kind of answer in the morning.

Sunday morning came quickly. After celebrating the 7 A.M. Mass, I headed back to the rectory with the meager collection. In the elegant dining room, Pastor Kane was already seated at the head of the table for an early breakfast with Father Gaughn and the weekend visitor, a priest of the Redemptorist order, who would celebrate the next Mass that morning instead of the pastor. I sat down across from the visitor. Everyone was sipping coffee and eating breakfast with little to say at such an early hour.

Margaret walked into the dining room from the kitchen with a plate of toast in one hand and a plate of crisp bacon in the other. She was visibly agitated and was direct in asking about what had happened the night before. “Did any of you hear all that racket last night? Good God, it sounded like all hell broke loose. I thought I was going to find a disaster in my kitchen. It sounded like someone broke every glass and dish at once! What in the name of Saint Patrick happened?” I could tell that her peace of mind required immediate, decisive answers to her questions.

“I heard it, too!” said Pastor Kane.

“So did I,” repeated the visitor.

As it turned out, everyone in the rectory had heard Saturday night’s commotion but had not dared to venture outside his or her room. Father Gaughn and I were not the only witnesses to sonic explosions and erupting noises.

“You all heard it, too?” I chimed in. “ Father Gaughn and I both ran down here to see what the racket was about, but found nothing. What the heck happened?”

“He must be at it again,” said the visitor.

“At it again? Who’s at it again?” Margaret and I asked, almost in unison.

“Muldoon, of course!” the visitor answered.

“Who the hell is Muldoon?” asked Father Gaughn.

“You’ve never heard of Muldoon? In this church? I thought everyone in the archdiocese knew this story. Well,” the visitor explained, “Bishop Muldoon was pastor of Saint Charles back in its heyday. He loved this place. The people here were very dear to him. Eventually, he was transferred to Rockford to establish a new diocese, but he always considered this rectory as his home. Muldoon actually helped design the church where you celebrated Mass this morning and had a crypt built behind the main altar. He wanted to be buried here, but, naturally, his body never made it out of Rockford. Rumor has it that his ghost came back and lives here today."

"So you believe that a ghost of a former bishop made all that commotion last night?" I asked.

"Well, I can't be positive, but I wouldn't doubt it. I mean, this isn't the first time that something like this has happened. This place is famous for ghost stories. Many of the old-timers I knew that lived here experienced their own ghost stories. I had a friend who was here during the time that Muldoon died, and he said that he started hearing all these crazy noises right away. The old-timers said that it was because of his ring."

"What do you mean? What ring?" I asked.

"The legend is that Muldoon willed his bishop's ring to the people of Saint Charles as his sign of affection and devotion for the parish. The ring never made it back here, and its absence caused all the ghostly happenings."

"Like what?" asked Father Gaughn.

"Some say they had seen Muldoon's ghost ascend the stairs to the second floor on his way to his old suite. Other priests say they heard sounds like furniture being moved back and forth on the hardwood floors of the third floor and banging against the walls. When they went to investigate, they found nothing wrong."

Pastor Kane interrupted, "I know one of the former pastors. He told me that, one day, he saw Muldoon come out of his bedroom. He was terrified! Put him right over the edge. He was already a drunk, but he drank even more so to help him deal with seeing a dead bishop."

Up to this time, Kane had said very little to anyone. But the pastor was easily drawn into the conversation that morning. There was no doubt Kane needed to control the table talk and was reluctant to have any priest, much less a visitor, steal his thunder. He barged in to tell what he knew of his predecessor, the ghostly Muldoon.

He continued, more excited than I'd ever seen him, pointing dramatically in my direction: "Then there's the room across from your sitting room, Rocco, that seems to be one of Muldoon's favorite haunting spots. Lights and radios have been going on and off there for years. If there is a ghost, he seems more mischievous than anything . . . ahhhh, it's probably just bad wiring."

"I wouldn't be so sure," commented the visitor, in a slightly flip manner as he continued to eat breakfast. "I've heard too many stories to just dismiss Muldoon's ghost. And I'd be careful, if I were you. He loved this place. You'd better treat his parish right. You don't want to be his target."

"Why? What else do you know about Muldoon?" I probed.

The visitor obviously knew the legend well and was sure that Muldoon was behind last night's antics. "Well, while Muldoon was in Chicago, he was chosen Archbishop Feehan's auxiliary bishop. And with that Muldoon made an undying enemy, Jeremiah J. Crowley. He was an Irish-born priest who despised Muldoon for being appointed over him. Crowley plagued and humiliated Muldoon for two decades. But that is another story in itself. I've got a Mass to say." Story time was over.

The Redemptorist's words intrigued me—I wanted to hear more. Meanwhile, Margaret was terrified. Right after Mass, the little Irish cook implored our clerical visitor to bless her room and her kitchen with holy water. The visitor dressed for the occasion in black cassock, white surplice, violet stole, and biretta, with the ritual in his left hand and the holy water aspergillum in his right hand. Margaret accompanied him, carrying the holy water vessel. She had him bless everything: her room, the stairways, the corridors, and the kitchen. What could it hurt? At least it would bring her some peace and comfort.

The very next morning, the kitchen was dark and quiet. No coffee. No breakfast. When we checked Margaret's room, we discovered that all of her personal possessions were gone. Leaving her ring of house keys on the kitchen table, Margaret had fled without a farewell to anyone. I never saw or heard from her ever again.

About a week later, and after a few more complaint sessions regarding Pastor Kane, Father Gaughn moved out quietly and without notice, in the same fashion as Margaret. Gaughn told me more than once that he would do something to free himself of such a dismal rectory and the control of Pastor Kane. It was all too much for a man of his sensitivity and idealism. He could not cope with a housekeeper who had full control or with the pastor's ineptness and lack of basic priestly ideals. Muldoon's haunting just must have been the straw that broke the camel's back. Unknown to the rectory staff, Gaughn must have worked out his problems with the chancery office. After only two months at Saint Charles, he was allowed to relocate himself not only in another parish but into another diocese altogether. Quietly and swiftly, Father Gaughn had left. Within my short time at Saint Charles, both the cook and the senior assistant dropped off the face of the earth—the only ones left were Pastor Kane, Irma, and myself.

∞

While gathering data for this book, I was able to track down "Father Gaughn." I wrote him a letter requesting any Muldoon recollections he might have to contribute to my book. Even after 40 years, Father Gaughn remembered me well. He sent back the letter I had written him, and in light and rambling scribbles he explained that he was very ill and was returning to the hospital. Within days of receiving his correspondence, I found out that Father Gaughn had passed away. With me, he had been a witness to Muldoon's sonic manifestation on a hot Saturday night in mid-August of 1956.

The strangest thing about that night is that I experienced it with so many other people. Generally, when you hear of ghost stories, they are told independently, experienced by individuals. As far as hauntings go, it's quite rare for a group of people to experience the same haunting.

For the life of me, I cannot find or remember the name of the visiting priest who relished telling the legend of Muldoon. He was an Irish priest of the Redemptorist community and older than 50 at the time, but his name eludes me. After hearing the Redemptorist's stories, I understood what Father Leo meant when he told me that strange things happen at Saint Charles Borromeo — that I'd understand once I'd been there awhile. Putting it all together, I surmised that Saint Charles was the rectory that Father Casey had spoken of at Quigley years before. Indeed, this must be it!

Chapter Six

The Curse of the Ring

THE WEEKS FOLLOWING THE departure of Father Gaughn proved to be lonely and unpleasant for me. Irma and Pastor Kane continued to be their aloof and impersonal selves, and I now had to do the work of two assistants. Besides having to pick up the slack, I now had no one left in the rectory to confide in or relate to on a daily basis.

Kane was visibly upset at the unexpected loss of his staff and took their abandonment personally. Denying that he was in any way responsible, Pastor Kane justified Father Gaughn's departure by blaming me, saying that Gaughn disliked working with Italians and that I had driven him from Saint Charles. But I knew better and managed to keep my perspective. When Kane called them "a couple of quitters," I couldn't help but chuckle to myself. I knew Margaret was a good and dutiful cook, and heaven knows that Father Gaughn tried to be the best priest he could at Saint Charles.

If anyone was a quitter, it would've been Kane—but even he couldn't be called a quitter because in order to quit, he first would've had to at least try. And I had yet to see any effort on his part to even try serving this blighted parish. Calling Kane a quitter—on the neighborhood, on his vocation as a priest, as a person with compassion for human suffering—would have been a compliment to him.

Although he remained generally remote, Pastor Kane started talking more and more about Muldoon. The ghostly bishop was one of the few things we could speak about that did not end up in a disagreement. After experiencing that unexplainable apparition a few weeks prior, I was intrigued about Muldoon and all the related ghost stories. Kane had the knowledge and experience of a previous generation and knew more inside facts about Muldoon's life and the legend of his ghost. Every now and then, Kane would speak during supper about what he knew of Muldoon, and I would learn a little bit more. Kane did not usually offer new information on Muldoon, but had to be prodded with leading questions on the topic. In the period before meals, when I was the only priest in the house, I would prepare questions about Muldoon to break the silence and gather extra details.

"It was all in that bishop's ring. It was bad luck for him the moment they put it on his finger at Holy Name Cathedral to the day he died in Rockford. That ring brought him only embarrassment and grief. It must have been cursed.

"Muldoon had nothing but problems after Feehan nominated him bishop. Then there was this Father Crowley from out in the sticks who drove himself crazy about Muldoon being appointed over him, especially because Muldoon was American-born and Crowley came straight from Ireland. Crowley was so bitter about being overlooked, he attacked the man's character with a vengeance. First he said that Muldoon was immoral and just plain inept. Then he called him a pitiful drunk. Then a pervert. It just got worse, and

The Episcopal Ring received by Peter J. Muldoon at his consecration, based on a drawing in the *Chicago Tribune*, July 21, 1901. (Illustration by David Facchini.)

worse, and worse. It was so embarrassing to both Muldoon and the Church! After awhile, people started believing there was something to Crowley's accusations. I don't think Muldoon's reputation ever fully recovered.

"Crowley went right off the deep end. Once he realized that his dream of advancing through the ranks was crushed, he just snapped! Eventually, he abandoned the priesthood and cut himself off from the Church. He became this avowed and bitter anti-Catholic writer. He even called himself 'the New Luther.' But Crowley was living in a dream world, and when he left the Church, his world just collapsed around him.

"In the meantime, some of the Irish-born priests turned on Archbishop Feehan. They were afraid that they were losing power in America. They were determined that one of their own should be Feehan's right-hand man. Muldoon's appointment really caused a rift between the Irish-born priests and the narrow backs." (*Narrow backs* was a term for the American-born clergy of Irish descent.) "Crowley's goal was to create chaos in the diocese, and he delivered.

"After Feehan died of a stroke, Quigley took over as archbishop and Muldoon was appointed to Rockford. By that time, Crowley was excommunicated. But it didn't matter. All of those accusations followed Muldoon there, too. That man got no rest until he died.

"Yep, that ring must have been cursed. I don't know and I don't care why that ring didn't make it back here. We sure don't need Muldoon's luck. It's probably a blessing it never made it back to Saint Charles."

Over time, Kane obsessed more and more about Muldoon. Some days, he would speak as if he were trying to logically explain some of the weird happenings in the rectory, like the sound of stomping and pounding when no one else was in the rectory, the rolling of dressers and cabinets on the wooden floors above us, or the cold pockets of air and gusts of wind blowing through the rectory that came out of nowhere. Other days, I could tell he was intimidated by the idea that a ghost was protecting Saint Charles.

As for me, I enjoyed learning more about Muldoon and hearing about the unexplainable occurrences that took place in the rectory and continued experiencing the unexplainable myself. I remember such things as the dense smell of hot tar that came and went without notice; pens and books disappearing and re-appearing on my desk; window shades rolled up with no one around; and the bottom sash of my bedroom window moved up (or down) when I was away from the room.

I was very surprised that I had never heard anything about Muldoon or the hauntings prior to my assignment. Priests are known to maintain an active and all-inclusive grapevine, and news of a haunting would have traveled fast. Usually, nothing escapes the network. I guess this news never made it down into the seminary. To my knowledge, no other rectory in Chicagoland was rumored to be haunted.

Late one evening, about a month or so after Father Gaughn had left, Pastor Kane was sitting snuggly in a barrel chair in the study of his suite, leaning back, lazily watching TV with Duke at his side. On the wall behind him hung a large oil painting, about three feet wide by four feet high, with a very heavy ornate, gold leaf, plaster frame that must have weighed at least 50 pounds. The painting was held securely to the wall on heavy-duty wire, anchored by two industrial bolts burrowed deep into the plaster wall. In the blink of an eye, both bolts popped out from the wall. The heavy painting swiftly slid down the plaster wall like the lead-bottomed blade of a guillotine, just missing the pastor's skull. The picture frame slammed down and shattered shards of hard plaster all over the room, gouging the hardwood floor.

"My God . . . it's Muldoon! He's out to get me!" cried Kane.

The crash and screaming spurred me to run from my own study to see what was the matter. Kane unlocked his door and stood in the open doorway trembling, looking back at the plaster mess on the floor, and seeing in the rubble his possible demise at the quick hand of the fearsome rectory ghost.

"Rocco, that painting just missed my head. He's out to get me! What if I was just two inches closer to the wall? I would have been killed, I tell you!"

Stepping into Kane's room, I looked up at the bare wall where the heavy painting had been hanging. There was no sign of the plaster wall crumbling or that the picture was hung improperly. The picture wire was perfectly intact, and the bolts that unexplainably shot out from their mountings were lying on the floor in good condition. Though I could not explain it, the occurrence looked planned and deliberate. I didn't know what to think about all of this ghost talk at this point. Maybe there was something to what the Redemptorist said: "I'd be careful, if I were you. He loved this place. You'd better treat his parish right." Maybe this was Muldoon's way of telling Pastor Kane that he'd better shape up. And though all these thoughts were crossing my mind in the few seconds as I assessed the mess in the pastor's sitting room, my natural instinct was to help Kane calm down. All this Muldoon talk was pushing him toward a breakdown.

"Now just relax! You're getting hysterical. No one is out to get you."

"No—I can tell he's out to get me! I can feel it. We are not the only priests living in this house." A look of pure horror was on the pastor's face as he pieced together the entire incident for me. Kane's flippant attitude toward the ghost of Bishop Peter J. Muldoon a few weeks prior had evolved into an intense fear that continued from that day forward.

The following day, Pastor Kane and Irma both searched for a way to appease the rectory ghost. They were both convinced that Muldoon was out to get Kane. Perhaps the threat of a ghost guarding the rectory returned Kane's conscience to him, making him recognize that he had not adequately served Saint Charles. Meanwhile, I thought the vengeance of Muldoon couldn't have been focused on a more appropriate target.

Searching the storage rooms on the third floor, Irma found a dusty old oil portrait of Bishop Muldoon, still in good condition and in a gold frame, about two feet square. Muldoon looked benign and content in his portrait, as if he had had a hearty meal and a glass of fine wine before sitting for the artist. His face looked as serene as the Mona Lisa; he had an Irish twinkle in his clear blue eyes. The anxious pastor blessed the painting and installed it ceremoniously on the outside wall of his suite, a prominent place where it would always be easily seen. The following day, Kane had the janitors place an oblong table along the wall under Muldoon's likeness and positioned a table lamp to continually illuminate his pleasant face. Kane had erected a shrine to placate the ghost of Muldoon, hopefully keeping his activity at bay.

By now, Muldoon had deeply impacted everyone I knew who lived in the rectory. He scared poor Margaret away and was too much for Father Gaughn. Pastor Kane and Irma were now living in a new state of fear. And I had witnessed it all. As dubious as it might have seemed, Muldoon was my only explanation for all the things that were happening. We all believed that there was an unseen presence in the house, and I was curious. Who was this man behind the ghost? What made his connection so strong that he would come back to haunt this rectory? And was I, a priest trained to believe in a spiritual afterlife, now believing in the existence of ghosts? There were a lot of missing pieces. At this time in my life, I did not realize that it would take me more than 40 years to collect and understand bits of information regarding the history of Chicago, Catholic dogma, ghost stories, and the lives of Muldoon and Crowley to puzzle together such a mosaic story.

∞

Like a wedding ring, the episcopal ring represents a deep and unending bond. It symbolizes the union between a bishop and the community he serves. On Sunday, July 21, 1901, the Chicago Daily Tribune featured an article titled "Rich Vestments and Insignia to Be Conferred upon Bishop Muldoon Thursday During His Consecration." Of the ring, the article stated, "The episcopal ring of solid gold set with Amethyst of three penny weights (weight of a silver penny) will be brought forth, blessed, and placed on the bishop's ring finger of the right hand. It is a symbol of fidelity."

Traditionally, when a priest is consecrated a bishop, he has the opportunity to design for himself a coat of arms and to pick out the ornamentation of his own vestments. Surprisingly, as a man of Irish heritage, Muldoon did not choose the traditional emerald. His ring and all of his other vestments — his pectoral cross, crosier (bishop's staff), mitre (bishop's hat) and matching maniple (a decoration of the wrist that is no longer worn), stole and chasuble—were encrusted with amethyst gems. Amethyst, the purple form of crystal quartz, is an intriguing stone found in some tombs of the pharaohs of ancient Egypt. The purple gems were used as a symbol of worthiness through which the deceased would merit conscious afterlife. Even to this day, the amethyst is seen as a powerful stone; it is often used by ghost seekers to help them induce psychic dreams of spirits. Just perhaps, of all the gems he could have chosen, Muldoon had his conscious afterlife in mind when he chose the amethyst.

Chapter Seven

The Conscious Afterlife

SO, WHAT DO YOU BELIEVE? Though my intention in writing this book is not to present a religious thesis on Christian immortality or an essay on the existence of heaven and hell, the topic of ghosts always questions one's personal beliefs of the afterlife. Atheists believe that this is it—there is no God and an afterlife is nothing but a self-serving concept to give human beings peace. Many cultures in India believe that the human spirit is reincarnated and born into another living form on earth. In Judaism the idea of immortality lies more in the reputation one builds through the good works that he or she has completed during a lifetime. And then there are many other cultures that believe in the conscious afterlife, that death is but a transition and from there, a person's soul is born into a living spirit world. Many world cultures, like the Egyptian and the Chinese, naturally came to believe in a conscious afterlife without the benefit of Christian

Scriptures. Then, the Good News of Christ's resurrection preached by apostles Peter and Paul to hopeless slaves of the Roman Empire led to the eventual collapse of a centuries-old power. God raised Jesus Christ from the dead—no other event or belief in all of human history has so changed the world. More than any other idea, the resurrection of Jesus and the Christian thought of human resurrection with Him continues to captivate a vast assembly believing in a conscious life after death. Each person reading this book knows he or she will one day die. So, in discussing the existence of ghosts and what happens to the human soul after death, what is it that you believe?

Personally, I broadly interpret the following words of the Apostles' Creed in understanding the concept of ghosts: "I believe in the Communion of Saints"—that intimate fellowship of the living and the dead—in union with Jesus Christ, bound by the power of the Holy Spirit. In a broad sense, "saints" describes all Christians, the living and the dead; in fact, it describes all of humanity. Consistent with the teaching of the creed is the seeing, hearing, and feeling of the spirits of those recently dead and of long ago—bound together as an unbreakable continuum down the corridors of centuries linking ancient and modern times. In a communion of saints, the living and the dead are all connected to one another.

In Christian belief, the resting place of the conscious afterlife is either heaven for those who have achieved salvation, hell for those who are eternally damned, or purgatory for those who have died with sin and are being cleansed before entering into the Kingdom of God. It's my belief that a ghost has not achieved any of these goals. The spirit, for some unexplainable reason, has not yet found peace in this life and continues to be bound to its earthly home. So it makes sense why the spirit of Bishop Peter J. Muldoon had not moved on to future rest. As a brother priest, Muldoon

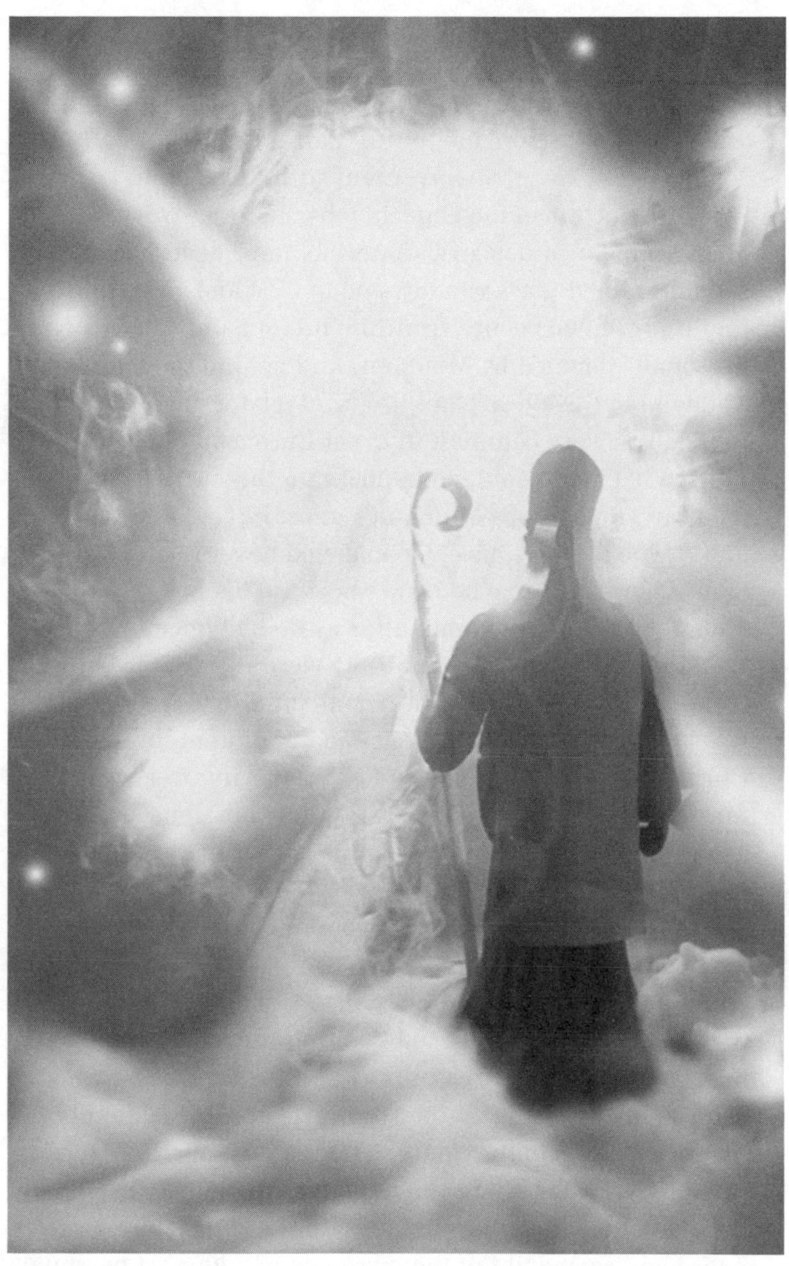

The Conscious Afterlife. (Illustration by David Facchini.)

was eternally linked to the clergy, a man of the Spirit connected to the ministry through grace and a conscious understanding of our communion. In addition to that bond, there was an even stronger tie to Saint Charles Borromeo. Muldoon had a deep involvement with this parish. He oversaw construction of the church, laboring over every element of the building's designs, materials, and decorations. The radiant stained-glass windows on its east and west transepts that represented scenes from the life of Saint Charles were personally donated by Muldoon. And behind the main altar, Muldoon set aside a place for a crypt for his own burial (which was very common in great European churches). He infused his heart, soul, and spirit into this sacred place and its future. So perhaps Muldoon's ghost lingered at Roosevelt and Hoyne because his episcopal ring never made it back to Saint Charles. Or maybe it was because his body was never entombed behind the main altar as he had once intended. I tend to believe that his hauntings were relevant to the protection of the parish. The church that he so loved was being threatened by Pastor Kane's abandonment of teaching Christ's Gospel. Maybe Muldoon was trying to redirect his former parish back on course to its holy mission. Or perhaps Muldoon was trying to warn the parish of its impending physical obliteration.

Eventually, I came to believe in a conscious connection between Muldoon and me. Sometimes, when I was alone, I could just sense that someone else was in the room. Or in the dark silence of the rectory on a Sunday night, I could hear someone else breathing. I recall the sound of heavy steps in the halls and on the stairs late at night when I knew no one else was in the house. Though it is one thing to simply tell a ghost story never having experienced an apparition, I believe it is a completely different matter to have heard and seen and felt the presence of a ghost. I personally have felt that conscious connection. As for the ghost of Peter J. Muldoon, I believe.

∞

The Christian religion is obviously not the only tradition that believes there is a connection between the living and the dead. Native Americans who lived in the Chicago region for uncountable ages demonstrated a conscious connection with the spirits of their ancestors. Although they left us with no printed history, we do have verbal knowledge of the ceremonial funeral practices of the local Fox and the Sac, and from them we can detect some common customs still in existence. Believing in the afterlife, Native Americans routinely placed gifts on a corpse to keep its ghost subdued and to be used on the spirit journey in the afterlife. Such gifts included fur skins, clothing, corn and other food, tools, pots, flint, arrowheads, feathers, and ornamental beads. In imitation of these ancient customs, I remember placing family photographs in my father's jacket pocket at his wake, along with religious medals and tokens. These meaningful gifts of love were, in essence, our family's accompaniments into my father's conscious afterlife.

The idea of placing gifts on a corpse eventually gave way to the common practice of placing flowers or flower petals into the new grave. In time, this routine led to the Christian custom of casting loose soil onto the coffin at the open grave with the Genesis admonition to the living, "Remember, man, thou art dust, and to dust thou shalt return."

Even the color black, now worn in respect for the dead, has interesting beginnings based upon the idea that malevolent ghosts were a threat to the living. The Indigenous peoples of South America were so afraid of the dead that even the most distant kin would take new names in the hope that the spirit would be unable to recognize and harm them. The color black was worn to disguise the living from the newly deceased. Eventually, wearing black by the family, mourners, undertakers, and pallbearers was meant to show respect. But originally, it was meant to keep those nearest to the corpse inconspicuous, to hide and protect the living from returning spirits.

Also note that in early funeral practices, there was no embalming. Outside of being ornamental, flowers were used to break the pervasive smell of death. The newly dead were to be buried as soon as possible. Wakes were short. There was to be no stopping the procession once it headed out to the cemetery, in order to bring eternal rest to the dead as soon as possible. This custom is followed even in our day, as the funeral cortege has the right of way in traffic.

These and many other funeral practices that are common today have evolved throughout the years from our fear of ghosts. Today, there might be a new understanding that these practices take place in respect of the life of the deceased. However, for the most part, traditions toward treating the dead haven't changed. The significance is this: Despite the lack of scientific evidence for the existence of ghosts and any religious refutation that ghosts exist in our physical realm, there has always been a natural human fear and curiosity of ghosts and the conscious afterlife. Though we might not actively realize it, that curiosity and fear is evident to this day in our customs. In the very least, it is apparent through our interest in ghost stories.

Chapter Eight

Chi-ca-gou: A Sacred Place

IMAGINE A SWAMP SITTING ON the southwestern banks of what we now know as Lake Michigan, famous for the wild onion and garlic that grew profusely on the shore of the freshwater lake and its many sandy tributaries. Before this area grew into the metropolis that we know today, before a man named Muldoon had the opportunity to add to the spiritual growth of the city, this was a vast and uncharted territory of bounty and beauty. It was a place of greatness, a sacred place that the Miami named Chi-ca-gou. Historians can trace its first inhabitants as far back as 6000 B.C. to the Illinois tribe. (*Illinois* means "real men.") The land was a boundless basin, plentiful with rivers and streams. It was an infinite plain of unending beauty, emitting the fresh perfume of onion and garlic and the sweet dampness of prairie grass. It was a widespread hunting ground wild with endless moose, deer, elk, ducks, geese, and turkeys—all provided by the grace of the Good Spirit. It was an untouched and unfinished country.

Nourished and awed by this fruitful land, the spiritual peoples that first lived here were fashioned by what they deemed a Good Spirit. In fact, they considered all the forces of nature—the wind, the rain, the sun, lightning, and thunder—to be spirits. By the greatness of the Good Spirit, many tribes gave thanks for the bounty of fish from the rivers and streams, the corn and grain from the fertile ground, and the meat and fur made available from hunting. There was also an Evil Spirit to which the tribes often gave gifts to keep it appeased. This great prairie was too immense to be subdued by the area's many tribes both large and small: Tamaroa, Iroquois, Miami, Ottawa, Wyandotte, Chippewa, Fox, Potawatomi, Illini, Sioux, Peoria, and Kaskaskia. All were conscious of the powerful natural forces of the sky, the water, and the soil. The Native Americans were astounded by the gifts of their generous and unseen Spirit. They were captivated by the endless beauty of the unshorn fields and lived free from the constraints of time measurement. Those who lived and died here during life's small cycle left virtually no mark or impression on the rich, untamed soil. To them, this place was truly consecrated ground—a hallowed place called Chi-ca-gou.

Chicago's modern history began in 1672, when the explorer Samuel de Champlain, headquartered in Quebec, Canada, commissioned Louis Jolliet and Father Jacques Marquette to expand the French empire by searching for a water route to the Pacific. Jolliet was a fur trader and explorer in his early twenties. Marquette was a Jesuit priest in his mid-thirties. Together they explored the Great Lakes region. Satisfied with their early discoveries, Marquette and Jolliet sought a great river that would take them to the Pacific Ocean. Through their journey, a young explorer craving furs and maps of new territories and a holy man seeking to evangelize Christ split an ancient wall that could never be resealed or restored. There was no turning back. The expe-

Painting of Pere Jacques Marquette, S. J. (Reprinted from *Diamond Jubilee of the Archdiocese of Chicago, 1920.*)

dition of Jolliet and Marquette would change the landscape of Chi-ca-gou forever.

On May 17, 1673, they embarked from Saint Ignace, a mission station near the Straits of Mackinac where the Lake of the Illinois (Lake Michigan) and Lake Huron are joined, and headed south. For food they carried smoked meat and corn. Along the way, they lived on corn meal boiled in the sweet sap of maple trees and feasted on the abundance of garlic and wild onions growing along the shoreline. They traveled in two large birch-bark canoes, each 30 feet in length, with five experienced voyagers and five Indians to help with moving the boats through cold and choppy waters and portaging supplies. Rather than cut across the frigid, violent lake and risk the quick destruction of such a light craft, the party paddled the two vessels along the western side of the lake to Green Bay, Wisconsin, to the Fox River, and to the Wisconsin River and then discovered the mighty

Mississippi. The expedition caught the speed and flow of the descending river that ran for hundreds of miles—not to the west but south to Mexico. Eventually realizing they were not finding the Northwest Passage to the Pacific and sensing imminent danger from Spanish soldiers and hostile warlike tribes of the southland, Marquette and Jolliet decided to turn back. Reversing their course, the men laboriously paddled their canoes north against the rushing current of the Mississippi until they reached Illinois, where the water flow moved them into the calmer Illinois River and into the land called Chi-ca-gou.

Marquette was the first known European to step onto Illinois soil when he disembarked from his canoe in Kaskaskia. Lovingly known as "the Black Robe" by the tribal peoples for the cassock he wore, Marquette looked to bring the many tribes of the area the Word of the Gospel. This missionary journey that taught of a life beyond the grave further sanctified this soil so revered by the American Indians. After four months, the explorers decided to return to Saint Ignace. On his trip north, Marquette preached the Gospel to the Kaskaskia and Peoria tribes and promised to return the following year. Through this first heroic mission, the Church had brought the teachings of Jesus Christ to an untouched territory.

Eventually, Jolliet and Marquette parted company. Jolliet returned to Montreal. On his way home, Jolliet's smaller canoe flipped over. Tragically, two of his rowers and a small boy given to him as a servant drowned. All his papers, maps, and journals sank to the bottom of the waters, lost forever. Jolliet was devastated by the loss of his precious documents. He never returned to France, and eventually, Jolliet died in Canada (in 1700).

As promised, Marquette made a return journey to visit the Kaskaskia and Peoria tribes in October of 1674. His holy journey was the first extended sojourn of white people within the limits of what is now known as the city of Chicago. On October 24, after visiting the Kaskaskia for a second time, he came to the Chicago River (near what is now State Street) and continued south, running parallel to the lake, until reaching the point where it empties into the lake. (Different historians believe Marquette's first camp was pitched somewhere near what is now known as Michigan Avenue and the east end of Madison Street, the current dividing line between the North and South Sides of Chicago.) From all appearances, the lakefront is the original site of the beginnings of Christianity in Chicago. Marquette celebrated Mass there on December 4, 1674.

In 1675 Father Marquette survived a brutal winter, what Chicagoans now call "character builders," in a crude trader's shelter on high ground along the Chicago River at Robey Street (now Damen Avenue), not far from what later became the territory of Saint Charles Borromeo parish. The stinging cold winds from the lake made him an isolated prisoner of the weather from November 1674 to March 1675. In this hut he administered the sacraments, said Mass, and taught the Indians about God and the paradise of heaven. By the end of the harsh winter, Marquette was wearing down. His bodily strength had been drained by the remote Indian way of life. Like the Indians around him, Marquette suffered from rheumatism from the extreme cold and eye inflammation from smoke in their tepees. And when there was nothing to eat, people either survived on tree bark or starved. On his way back to Saint Ignace in May of 1675, Marquette died of a gastrointestinal infection on the sandy beach of Ludington, Michigan. He was only 38.

In 1688, less than 15 years after Marquette's early death, a European mapmaker by the name of Franquelin officially designated this remote area Fort Chi-ca-gou, which was the spelling most frequently used by Native Americans and French traders in the New World. Many others used the spelling Che-cau-gou. The Chicago area was virtually dormant and undeveloped for another 100 years. In 1784 a Catholic Haitian named Jean Baptiste Pointe du Sable settled in an isolated fur-trading post, becoming the area's first "official" settler. Then on August 3, 1795, after losing the Battle of Fallen Timbers, the Potawatomi and other smaller tribes ceded six and a half square miles at the mouth of the Chicago River to General "Mad" Anthony Wayne, giving Americans complete control of the Northwest Territory. Thus began a blossoming and development of the region, and by 1803 the newly constructed Fort Dearborn stood on high ground at the intersecting points of the Chicago River and Lake Michigan.

Between 1810 and 1900, Chicago would experience tremendous, unprecedented growth. Chicago was growing in power and influence. Because of the fertile soil, access to waterways, and emerging railroads, many immigrants moved to Chicago in search of work. The vast area surrounding the city center, the unlimited prairie of swampy plains, soon began to sprout numerous wooden houses for the overwhelming numbers of the working class. Factories, stores, warehouses, schools, and churches encroached on every bit of open space. In 1847 Chicago was officially deemed a town, and by 1850 it had reached the status of city. The Near West Side of Chicago, with "Mother Halsted Street" as its open door, became the port of entry for immigrants: Germans, Irish, Poles, Italians, Greeks, Bohemians, Jews, and a host of smaller groups, each separated from one another along cultural, ethnic, and religious lines. It was a true melting pot. By the end of the nineteenth century, this frontier settlement of about 100 people would grow to a population of 1,688,575, more than 600,000 of those being Roman Catholic immigrants mainly from Europe. It was during this time of tremendous growth for Chicago that the Catholic Church in the United States would bloom, making Chicago one of the largest archdioceses in the world.

Today, at the south end of the Michigan Avenue bridge, over the Chicago River at Wacker Drive, is a monument signifying the approximate location of the original Fort Dearborn. (Photo by David Facchini.)

The first great migration began with the Germans in 1840, which brought countless Catholics from Bavaria and the Rhineland to the Chicago area seeking refuge from the persecutions of their homeland. Immigrants spurred by major economic and political upheavals in Germany were among the first to pour into the city and became Chicago's largest white ethnic group at the time. The efficient and well-organized Germans formed new, large parish complexes built around the parochial school. They erected massive and triumphant churches, like Saint Michael's in Old Town and Saint Alphonsus in Lakeview, which were coupled with schools, convents, and occasionally a brothers' house or high school. From these complexes would grow athenaeums for theater groups, bowling alleys, credit unions—almost every kind of human activity would be covered by the ecclesiastical umbrella.

The Irish, like the Germans before them, were next to saturate the city landscape, seeking out the treasures they were deprived of in Ireland: elusive liberty, economic security, and a bright future for their children. Immigrants came in waves of thousands responding to the overwhelming privations of rampant hunger from the potato famine, homelessness, and deepest poverty—results of the heavy hand of 700 years of English oppression. Many of them arrived on the scene in 1847, crossing the Atlantic in "coffin ships" just in time to work on the Illinois and Michigan Canal, while others grasped for any kind of work available, such as in construction, on the docks, or in meatpacking plants. But despite their many privations, the Irish had a great advantage over most other newcomers because they spoke English. In addition, the Irish were adept at politics, having honed these skills in battling for Catholic emancipation in Ireland and in repealing the forced union of the small countries of the British Isles. In just 50 years, by the end of the nineteenth century, the Irish advanced noticeably to the most skilled ranks that lived in every Chicago neighborhood. They became dominant in City Hall, Chicago politics, and police and fire departments and abundant in the Catholic priesthood, especially in the chancery office.

Because the severe English oppression denied Ireland of many human essentials, most native Irish traditions were lost. Almost immediately and naturally, their Catholic faith became their primary source of tradition, showing itself in the significant rites of passage of life: baptism, communion, confirmation, marriage, and the funeral. These bare essentials were sacred to the Irish, and they risked everything to preserve them. Missionary priests, like “holy tramps,” followed Irish Catholic settlers wherever they ventured, including Chicago. Also like the Germans, the Irish wisely built their own parish communities, such as Old Saint Patrick on Desplaines Street and Holy Family on Roosevelt Road—all developing from the Catholic grammar schools.

The Poles responded similarly to the heady freedom of proclaiming their free faith to the world, forming another Catholic community, whose native tongue was Polish. Poland, occupied for nearly 125 years by the Russians, Prussians, and Austrians, erupted into a massive flight of thousands to America with a mass concentration in Chicago. The Poles hungered for total liberation from overpowering and crushing neighboring countries. For the sake of newfound opportunities and precious income in America, Polish peasants filled factories, mills, and slaughterhouses with eager and enthusiastic workers. The fervent Poles fashioned massive, sacred spaces, like Saint Stanislaus Kostka—the largest Polish Roman Catholic church in the world, then reputed to be the Mother Church of all Polish Roman Catholics in Chicago. All Catholics of the Latin rite, and other Catholic rites of the East—the Belarusian, Ruthenian, Ukrainian, Chaldean, Maronite, Syro-Malabar, Syro-Malankar, and others—were in the conflicting weave of a

General Giuseppe Garibaldi, military leader of the Italian reunification, dissolving the Papal States in 1870. (Reprinted from www.redemptorist.org.)

vast and diverse tapestry of Catholic cultures emerging in Chicago's churches.

The Germans, the Irish, and the Polish came from similar situations of oppressive political and religious enemies and were seeking new opportunities in addition to the freedom of religious expression. But in Italy, Catholicism, the official state religion, preyed on its own people and had done so since the Edict of Milan in A.D. 325. The Papal States were formed in the late 700s and controlled most of Italy for centuries. There, the throne and altar were one. The Catholic Church was often the principal landlord and oppressor of its own people for some 1,000 years, until the Italian Unification under Giuseppe Garibaldi in 1870. Under severe papal rulers and their clerics, the poor were systematically kept uneducated, possessionless, wrongfully imprisoned, or tortured—and in many cases were executed. As a result, immigrants who fled Italy often bitterly resented the Church. So what mattered most to the Italian immigrants in America was not the politics of the Church or clerical bickering for position and power. Their basic interest was the daily workings of *la famiglia*, the obligations of being morally good, honest, and loving. With these core values, the immigrant Catholic Italians usually kept to themselves, living outside the reaches of the institutional ecclesiastical structure.

Incoming immigrant Italians, although universally baptized and coming from a Catholic nation, seldom attended Mass or went to the parochial schools, and only a small number became priests or nuns. The Italians were still suspicious of the Church and wanted little to do with Catholicism in America. This bothered American bishops, mostly Irish, who were unfamiliar with the Italian immigrants' experience back in Italy. The Third Plenary Council of Baltimore of 1884 discussed the problem of immigrant Italians who were Catholic only in name and chose to keep it that way. Ignorant of the ancient thought of the incoming Italians, this council paid scant attention to a long history of clerical abuse and human obstruction. The mostly Irish bishops felt the base of the "Italian problem" was one of language. But with the Italians the problems were deeper.

Fanning out from Halsted Street, the Germans settled along Lincoln Avenue, the Poles along Milwaukee Avenue, the Italians along Grand Avenue, and the Irish in Bridgeport and just about everywhere else (which is reflective of many of Chicago's neighborhoods to this day). Yet even in a new country, with the freedom to live and worship as they pleased, immigrants were never completely free of their past. Family members still lived across the Atlantic, and each national group carried its own emotional baggage from the old days in the old country. Truly, the strength of the immigrant Catholic Church in America was molded by this psychology of oppression, and the larger Catholic community was split by each nationality. This influx of strong, vibrant, and opposing national Catholic groups arriving in Chicago all at the same time would become the burden of men like Archbishop Feehan and his auxiliary bishop, Muldoon. The newcomers' vast numbers and varied needs and problems were compounded by the strong rivalry, stiff competition, and deep bitterness each national group held toward outsiders.

∞

Both of these things—the spirit of the tribal peoples who believed the swamplands of Chi-ca-gou to be sacred soil and the population boom that began with the frontiersmanship of Marquette—set the stage for the growth of the Catholic Church in the United States, which is one of the outstanding religious developments in American history. Contributing to this development was Muldoon, who had the vision to help grow the Chicago area and cultivate a Catholic population that, at one time, became the largest Catholic archdiocese in the world. With men like Damen and Feehan, Muldoon would erect magnificent places of worship, including Saint Charles, on what was considered worthless marshland. In retrospect, I guess it's no coincidence that, in popular ghost lore, swamps and marshes are considered breeding grounds for ghosts and hauntings.

Chapter Nine

Damen, Feehan, Henneberry, and Gill

BY 1835 TRIBAL PEOPLES WERE evacuated from Illinois, their place of origin, never to return or reclaim their vast territories. Earlier, in 1803, the idea of this type of ethnic cleansing was proposed by Thomas Jefferson; it eventually became national policy through the Indian Removal Act of 1830. Systematically, all local Native Americans were moved to reservations west of the Mississippi River. Like mist in the morning sunlight, the myriad of tribes, great and small, quickly evaporated from the area. With this removal, towering leaders of might and great wisdom—Che-ca-gou of the Micihegua, Sauk Chiefs Black Hawk and Keokuk, Shabbona, Tecumseh, and Sauganash—disappeared. To fill this void came thousands of immigrants led by a new breed of Illini, or "real men." There were now new heroic and energetic leaders who developed Chicago—predecessors and contemporaries who inspired the work of Peter J. Muldoon.

In 1926 the name of Robey Street was changed to Damen Avenue to memorialize the achievements of Reverend Arnold J. Damen, S.J., a pioneer educator and builder who in 1857 established Holy Family parish at 1080 W. Roosevelt Road as the first of three Jesuit parishes in Chicago. Damen came to Chicago from Saint Louis on a speaking engagement and attracted the attention of the Right Reverend Anthony O'Regan, Chicago's ordinary, who offered Father Damen an unfinished cathedral in the most promising and prosperous part of the city for a parish. Instead, Damen selected a new location on the West Side where large numbers of Irish Catholic immigrants were establishing their homes. Just as Marquette had opened the Chicago territory to European civilization in 1674, Damen would open the marsh and swamps to thousands of poor Irish immigrants. The small frame Holy Family Church was dedicated at 12th and May Streets in 1860 and was enlarged six years later.

Arnold J. Damen, S. J. helped establish Holy Family parish based upon the importance of parochial and secondary education. (Reprinted from *Diamond Jubilee of the Archdiocese of Chicago, 1920*.)

Though Damen was the brick-and-mortar founder of this new and massive Irish parish, he was better known as a pioneer of Catholic education. He worked long hours to open small satellite schools on the wide-open prairies everywhere west of Holy Family. In 1870 Damen established a school of higher education for boys, named after the founder of the Jesuit order, Saint Ignatius of Loyola. Damen's zeal and foresight in education was lauded throughout the diocese. Twenty years later, Holy Family became the largest Catholic parish in the entire United States, with 23 priests, 25,000 parishioners, more than 5,000 students at five grade schools, the celebrated Saint Ignatius High School, and a college that would eventually grow to become Loyola University of Chicago. On January 1, 1890, Father Arnold Damen died in retirement at Creighton University in Nebraska, far removed from the legacy he established in Chicago.

Rumor has it that the original church of the Holy Family, now a historic landmark, was built on the site of an ancient Indian cemetery; some argue that is was an old Indian battleground. Coincidentally, it is one of the few buildings to survive the Great Chicago Fire of 1871. Located at Roosevelt Road and Blue Island Avenue, just blocks southwest of the source of the citywide conflagration, Holy Family Church could have been immolated and reduced to ashes as was most of Chicago. As fate would have it for the parish, a strong wind rushing from the southwest pushed the towering flames east, saving the church. Had the wind been stagnant or blown to the west, the church would not have survived.

On Sunday night, October 8, 1871, Chicago was in the middle of a drought. There had been no rain for weeks. A relatively small population of about 300,000, a majority of them working-class people, lived in the parched wooden city. Though some commercial buildings had iron or brick facades, most residences were unpainted wooden houses and shacks. In fact, most of Chicago's building materials came from trees, the result being that Chicago was full of

Memorial site of the Great Chicago Fire of 1871. (Photo by David Facchini.)

wooden churches, wooden sidewalks, wooden fences, and wooden barns. Even the bridges that crossed the Chicago River were built of wood. As the story goes, Mrs. O'Leary's cow kicked over a lantern in a small barn located near the corner of DeKoven and Clinton, igniting the city. (The story may be fictional, but the location is accurate.)

The conditions were perfect for the fire, which started at 9 P.M., when most people were easing into sleep with a Monday workday ahead of them. The dry winds blowing at 35 miles per hour swept the fire eastward until it reached the lake. Then the wind-fueled fire spread north along the lakefront, engulfing everything in sight—homes, churches, stores, and schools. An hour and a half later, the fire department had already given up. The raging blaze overwhelmed the firefighters' limited resources, and almost instantly, block after block was swept up in apocalyptic flames. By 1:30 A.M. towering tongues of fire had reached the Chicago River, burning the State Street bridge and the area north of the river, including its luxurious homes. By 3 A.M. the pumps at the Chicago Avenue waterworks had collapsed in exhaustion. The Gothic, yellow-stone water tower and pumping station at Chicago and Michigan Avenues were the only structures intact for miles around. The Great Chicago Fire ultimately burned out an area of four square miles, from Taylor Street north to Fullerton Avenue, from Lake Michigan west to Halsted Street. The fire raged for a little more than a day, until the early morning of October 10, when rain began to fall. But by then, there was simply nothing remaining to burn. Left in the charred puddles of rain was a blackened wasteland of 300 dead men, women, and children and about 100,000 homeless Chicagoans. Property loss was estimated at $100 million. The inexorable and intense flames brought profound human misery on the city.

To the Catholic Church, the destruction that conservatively destroyed more than 20 of the Church's ecclesiastical structures, including Holy Name Cathedral, was enormous. The collective labor of thousands of dedicated workers who had constructed churches, convents, and schools was brought to naught in 27 hours. Thus it became a time to rebuild. Ashes and rubble would be swept as landfill into the swamps of Chicago to provide a solid foundation for future buildings. The City Corp of Engineers also dredged the Chicago River, making the waterway more navigable and using the silt, clay, and stone to help with the landfill project. This time around, construction would entail the use of fire-resistant brick and stone instead of combustible wood. Enter Archbishop Patrick A. Feehan from the Nashville Diocese, a priest with a solid reputation for post–Civil War reconstruction throughout a diocese that embraced the entire state of Tennessee. After years of effective planning and solid results in resurrecting his former battle-scarred diocese, Feehan had similar plans for restoring Chicago's burned-out churches, schools, and institutions and for building new parishes, which would serve the spiritual needs of the thousands of immigrants flooding the Chicago territory.

As a young man, Patrick Feehan attended Maynooth, the great export seminary of Maynooth, Ireland, which had the express purpose of preparing priests for service in distant lands, such as the missionary United States. In 1850 Feehan left Ireland for America in response to a call from the bishop of Saint Louis, Missouri. Young Feehan arrived as an ordained deacon and was ordained a priest on November 1, 1852. For the next 13 years, Father Feehan served as an assistant pastor, a seminary professor, and an administrator of the major seminary in Saint Louis.

In 1865 the Diocese of Tennessee had become vacant. Throughout the Civil War, Tennessee was a military highway for the advancing armies of both the North and the South; because of this, it was the stage for some of the war's bloodiest battles: the Battles of Fort Donelson on the Cumberland, Fort Henry on the Tennessee, Shiloh, Franklin,

Patrick J. Feehan was appointed Chicago's first Archbishop, September 1, 1880. (Reprinted from *Diamond Jubilee of the Archdiocese of Chicago, 1920.*)

Stones River, Lookout Mountain, Missionary Ridge, Chattanooga, and Nashville. By the end of the war, the state was virtually demolished, and the diocese found itself left with three priests, destroyed churches, and unending debt. Feehan spent 15 years rebuilding and resurrecting the Nashville Diocese, like a phoenix, from its own ashes.

To the disappointment of his congregation in Tennessee, Feehan was appointed to Chicago on September 1, 1880, becoming the city's first archbishop. Chicago was already in the throes of recovery from the fire by that time, and there was the need for a brick-and-mortar prelate to restore and expand the reach of the Catholic Church. Through Archbishop Feehan, numerous churches sprouted in the fields, first beginning with small and crude makeshift chapels and eventually expanding to great triumphal structures on the flat and open prairie.

In the meantime, Father Damen's Holy Family parish was going through a transition of its own. The more affluent

Father Francis S. Henneberry formed St. Pius V parish at 19th and Ashland. (Reprinted from *Diamond Jubilee of the Archdiocese of Chicago, 1920*.)

Father Patrick D. Gill, first pastor of St. Charles Borromeo. (Reprinted from *Silver Jubilee: Saint Charles Borromeo: 1885–1910.*)

Father Gill performed the first Mass for St. Charles in this storefront building, also known as "Ryan's Castle." (Reprinted from *Silver Jubilee: Saint Charles Borromeo: 1885–1910.*)

families of Holy Family parish left the neighborhood and began moving westward to untouched territories away from the devastation of the fire. Replacing them in the community along Taylor Street were primarily Italians from Southern Italy and Russian Jews. Additionally, as gentrification moved people away from the settled city, Archbishop Patrick A. Feehan opened the vacant western plains and grasslands to new holy sites, one being a new parish about a mile west of Holy Family at 2060 W. Roosevelt Road—Saint Charles Borromeo.

Like the founding of Holy Family, the beginning of Saint Charles Borromeo parish started with another pioneer of Catholic education. Father Francis S. Henneberry was pastor of the recently formed Saint Pius V Church at 19th and Ashland. He provided direction to the endless waves of immigrants pouring into the evolving area on what was deemed a worthless prairie on the western edge of the city limits. The developing plains were immense and lonely. However, a growing number of pioneers who chose to settle there found the grassland soil rich for farming. Word of the vast, fertile soil spread quickly, and soon newcomers from every location moved to this fresh new land in hopes for a prosperous future. No land in the Old Country proved to be as rich in earth as the flat, treeless prairies of the developing Chicagoland. By 1880 the oceans of wild grass were replaced by corn and wheat fields and an increasing number of German and Irish immigrants who continued to develop the area. The fruit of their labor was the emergence of small communities with small developing schools that formed the nucleus of the emerging parish complex. With this growth, it was apparent that another new parish was desperately needed. In 1885 Henneberry petitioned Archbishop Feehan for a new parish on behalf of this new community. Archbishop Feehan responded favorably to Father Henneberry's petition. For its name, Feehan selected Saint Charles Borromeo, a prelate widely known for his reforms of errant clergy and for reconstituting the Roman Catholic Church after the tragic Protestant breakaway.

In August of 1885, Feehan appointed Father Patrick D. Gill from his own chancery as the first pastor of the newly formed English-speaking parish. Gill did not have a church, convent, or school. But he did have a large expanse of land that was once highly revered by the area's tribal peoples, the strong beginning of satellite grade schools first established by Henneberry, and a waiting Catholic population anxious to be formed into a parish. During the earliest days of the formation of the Saint Charles parish, Father Henneberry provided lodging for Father Gill at Saint Pius. Before an actual church was erected, Father Gill celebrated Mass in a small commercial building called Ryan's Castle, named after its owner.

Father Gill worked quickly to build a church and in a short time constructed a preliminary combination brick building that housed a meeting hall in the basement, the church on the first floor, and classrooms and a convent on the second floor. After construction of the starter church, Pastor Gill turned his attention to building a permanent rectory, which was erected in 1891 and would house the many priests who followed him. In 1895 Father Peter J. Muldoon, secretary to Archbishop Feehan and chancellor of the archdiocese, replaced Father Gill, becoming the second pastor at Saint Charles. Father Gill was reassigned to construct the magnificent Our Lady of Mount Carmel Church on Belmont Avenue west of Broadway in Chicago's Lake View neighborhood, where he served as pastor for 20 years. On March 19, 1917, Father Gill's health began to fail, and after an illness of seven years, he died on January 4, 1924.

These four men—Damen, Feehan, Henneberry, and Gill—and the decisions they made regarding the Roman Catholic expansion in Chicago significantly impacted the work of Father Muldoon in building a new church for the

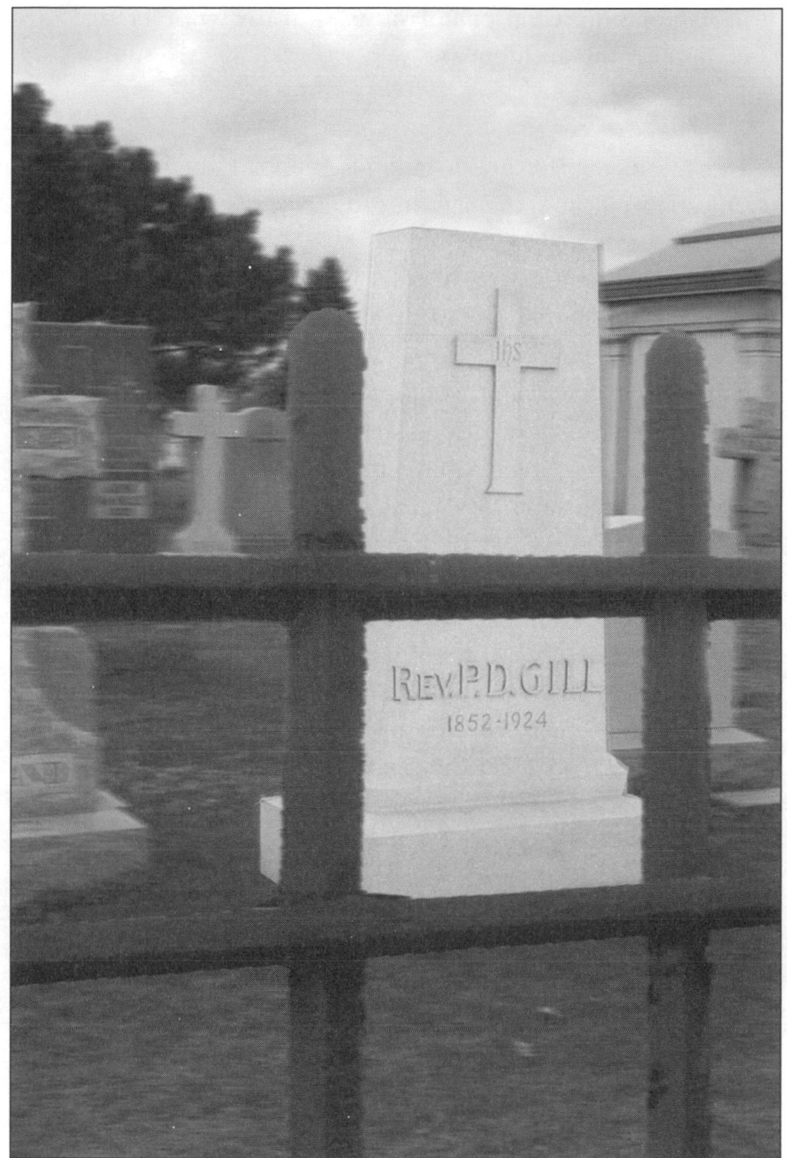

The tombstone of Reverend P. D. Gill in Calvary Cemetery as seen from Sheridan Road in Evanston, Illinois. (Photo by David Facchini and Marko Kevo.)

parish of Saint Charles Borromeo and his work as auxiliary bishop for the archdiocese.

∞

The mention of P.D. Gill reminds me of Calvary Cemetery, Chicago's oldest archdiocesan cemetery, purchased by Bishop Van De Velde in 1851 at $20 an acre. Bishop Duggan opened the new cemetery in 1859—120 beautiful acres spread between the border of Chicago and Evanston separated from the lake by Sheridan Road. Calvary is a historical Catholic cemetery, the burial place of many prominent figures through Chicago history. Archbishop Patrick A. Feehan was interred there until 1912, when his remains were transferred to the Bishops' Mausoleum at Mount Carmel Cemetery in Hillside, which was erected and put to use by Archbishop James Quigley in that same year.

Through my work as a realtor, I drove past Calvary Cemetery hundreds of times as I conducted regular business in Evanston. Driving south on Sheridan Road one spring afternoon, with the cemetery to my right, I noticed a large tombstone a few rows from the roadway that snatched my immediate attention with the simple inscription of "Reverend P.D. Gill." I hadn't seen that name for more than 40 years, only remembering it from the old baptism records stored at Saint Charles. Noticing the gravestone, I realized that I was probably one of only a few men alive who would recognize that name, and the chances of me spotting that name from a passing car seemed to be a million to one. Finding myself in the middle of a remarkable twist of fate, I turned in to the cemetery, found his gravesite, and said a silent prayer for Father Gill. I am still not sure how I noticed that specific tombstone from a moving car that day, and I guess I just followed my intuition through Calvary's labyrinth of gravesites to find his plot and say a prayer for him. In reflecting upon that experience today, as I write this book, I think that spotting Father Gill's tombstone was more than just a fluke.

Chapter Ten

The Life of Muldoon

BEFORE THE GHOSTLY LEGEND began, there was a man named Peter J. Muldoon. His life story starts with his immigrant parents. His father, John, was from County Caven, Ireland, and his mother, Catherine Coughlin Muldoon, came from County Galway. Like thousands of other immigrants facing starvation, religious persecution, and civil oppression in Europe, the teenage couple sailed for three months across the Atlantic in a deadly coffin ship, seeking a land of promise in America. They traveled with Catherine's brother, Father John Coughlin, who was a missionary priest always seeking new evangelical challenges. The trio bypassed the major immigration centers like New York and Chicago to settle in California. They chose Columbia in Tuolumne County, a small mining town east of San Francisco in the gold rush range of the Sierra Madre Mountains that offered quick and plentiful labor to immigrants. As often happens with young

Father John Coughlin, uncle and mentor to Peter J. Muldoon. (Reprinted from *Silver Jubilee: Saint Charles Borromeo: 1885–1910.*)

married couples, Catherine soon had a child, on October 10, 1862—an American-born son they named Peter. Peter later became the older brother to five other children: John, Mary, Ellen, Esther, and Irene. Eventually, John and Catherine Muldoon moved their young family to nearby Stockton, California, where the entrepreneurial John made a name for himself as a dependable and prosperous contractor.

By 1877 Peter had completed his education in public schools; it was time to consider higher education. It was decided that Peter would attend Saint Mary's College in Kentucky, where his uncle, John Coughlin, was already a teacher and member of the faculty. Father Coughlin was a strong force in Peter's life, and living near each other strengthened their lifelong relationship. Once Peter was in Kentucky, the uncle and nephew sought out each other's company whenever possible. Peter spent much of his free time accompanying Father Coughlin on his many works as a priest. During that time, Father Coughlin worked throughout the southern region, eventually met the young Bishop Feehan, and helped serve the desperate Tennessee Diocese. As for Peter, he enjoyed assisting his uncle in apostolic work, so it was no surprise that he also wanted to become a priest. In 1881, after college, Peter entered the well-known Saint Mary's Seminary in Baltimore, Maryland. (Saint Mary's closed its doors soon after the Second Vatican Council because of the decline of vocations in the United States.) After five years of final preparations, the theology student was ordained to the diocesan priesthood by John Loughlin, first bishop of Brooklyn, New York, in the Cathedral of Saint James on December 18, 1886. Peter was just 24 years old.

During the time Peter was in the seminary, Father Coughlin and Bishop Feehan had become good friends while working together in Tennessee. So when Feehan became archbishop in 1880, Father Coughlin moved to Chicago and eventually accepted a position as pastor of Our Lady of Lourdes on Chicago's North Side. After Peter was ordained in 1886, the young priest decided to follow his mentor-uncle. With a strong endorsement, Father Muldoon applied to Archbishop Feehan and was readily accepted as a candidate for the priesthood in Chicago. The young Irish-American priest received a strong first assignment at Saint Pius V parish in the Pilsen neighborhood, working with an exemplary pastor, Father Francis S. Henneberry. Life in the new parish pleased the boyish-looking priest. He worked well with his pastor and, as importantly, he was well liked and highly regarded by his new community. By way of Kentucky and Maryland, the Californian made Chicago his new home.

Father Muldoon quickly made a name for himself in Chicago. Working with a forward-thinking pastor, Muldoon soon built an enviable reputation throughout the archdiocese as a natural leader who had shown himself to be malleable and creative in working with his congregation at Saint Pius V. He was talented, prayerful, and knowledgeable, as

Rev. Peter J. Muldoon's first appointment as an assistant priest was at St. Pius V under the direction of Pastor Henneberry. (Reprinted from *Souvenir of the Archdiocese of Chicago, Commemorating the Installation of the Most Reverend George W. Mundelein, D.D. February 19, 1916.*)

well as being an insightful orator. He attracted attention from parishioners and other priests alike. Muldoon stood out. In less than a year and a half, Father Henneberry was duly notified that his popular young assistant would be transferred to the Archdiocesan Chancery Office as chancellor and secretary to the archbishop. This was quite a prestigious appointment for a 26-year-old man ordained less than two years. For Father Muldoon, it was the opportunity of a lifetime.

Muldoon moved to the archbishop's residence on State Parkway across from Lincoln Park and was ever at Feehan's side. As secretary, Muldoon was privy to virtually all of the archdiocese's private business, and as chancellor, he was instrumental in assisting the archbishop in the planning and building of many of the 140 churches erected during Feehan's tenure—more than any other bishop ever in

Chicagoland. To lighten the archbishop's workload, Muldoon was dispatched to numerous church dedications and blessings—one of which took place on October 8, 1892, at Our Lady of Lourdes on Ashland Avenue, where his uncle was the founding pastor. By reputation, the young chancellor was easy to work with, being both firm and flexible at the same time. The well-organized Muldoon was also bright, talented, and on top of his job. Holding these varied positions, Muldoon was exposed to all the details and the inner workings of running the archdiocese, and he eventually became a confidant whom Feehan could rely upon and trust—his right-hand man.

∞

In March of 1963, the archdiocesan newspaper of Chicago, the New World, published a piece about the last living member of the Muldoon family, Peter's sister Irene, entitled "Chicago Pays Last Tribute to Nun, 95." It followed with another short article of the sister's remembrances, with special attention to her deceased brother. Segments of both pieces were printed as follows:

> Chicagoans, particularly friends of the Religious Sisters of Mercy, this week mourned the death of one of the city's oldest nuns, Sister M. Irene Muldoon, who served all her religious life, 71 years, in the Chicago area.
>
> Sister M. Irene, 95, died Monday (March 4) at Mercy Infirmary, 620 Belmont Avenue, where she had lived for the past 12 years. She was a sister of the late Peter J. Muldoon of Rockford and earlier auxiliary of Chicago.
>
> Sister recalled the early days. . . . She remembered her brother, the First Bishop of Rockford, had received his early education in California, and later

The Cardinal's residence, as first constructed by Archbishop Feehan, located at State Parkway and North Avenue. (Reprinted from *Diamond Jubilee of the Archdiocese of Chicago, 1920*.)

Saint Mary's Seminary, Baltimore. She spoke of his ordination in 1886. She told little of herself but surely, in her memory, significant dates in her life must be intertwined with the events of her brother's life.

In 1895, only a year before Sister Irene's profession as a Sister of Mercy, Father Muldoon, then chancellor of the Chicago Archdiocese, was appointed pastor of Saint Charles Parish on the city's west side. The Irish immigrants who were his parishioners have given way to the latest arrivals, olive skinned newcomers from Mexico and Puerto Rico, and southern Negroes seeking livelihood in Chicago's factories. The neighborhood has changed but Saint Charles still stands as it did in the days of Bishop Muldoon . . . a testimony of Christ's love for all men.

Her bond with diocese of Rockford was strongly formed and on the day of the Jubilee Mass, the Most Reverend John J. Boylan, Bishop Muldoon's second successor was in the sanctuary of Saint Patrick's Academy.

During Bishop Loras Lane's (later) visit with Sister Irene . . . Sister looked thoughtfully at the ring worn by Bishop Lane. As he answered her questions about the growth of the diocese, she was evidently pleased. An onlooker may have detected an air of justifiable pride as she thought of her brother who had also worn a Bishop's ring.

Chapter Eleven

Building on Holy Ground

THE FEEHAN LEGACY LEFT AN indelible mark on Chicago. Most noticeably, Feehanville (which is now known as Maryville Academy) and much of the city's ecclesiastical beauty can be traced back to the construction of churches during the late 1800s. In creating these numerous churches and institutions, Archbishop Feehan used the concept of national parishes. To reflect a Catholic presence in different neighborhoods, which are greatly based upon nationality in Chicago, Feehan fostered the construction of churches that maintained the culture of different ethnic groups, no matter how large or small. The Germans had Holy Trinity, the Poles had Saint Stanislaus Kostka, and Our Lady of the Assumption was for the Italians. Priests who spoke the language and shared the culture of the immigrant population served each parish. Feehan was also wise enough to construct his advisory council of priests from the chief immigration groups. His aim was to preserve the constant legacy of the Catholic faith and a defined universal teaching in conjunction with meeting the independent needs of each national group. Through creative ideas such as this, the Catholic Church catered to the needs of Chicago's diverse populations—and grew.

With the new construction, Feehan realized that the diocese was significantly understaffed. There were simply not enough priests in Chicago to meet the needs of the booming parishes. During his tenure, Feehan kept up by ordaining more than 250 priests, which is an amazing achievement in itself. But the American crop of priests still was not enough. He needed more personnel to meet Chicago's burgeoning demands. Feehan turned to his alma mater, the seminary of Maynooth, for help, and Ireland responded with many good priests who came overseas to serve in Chicago. However, many an Irish bishop also took this opportunity to dump alcoholics, dissidents, and troublemakers with emotional and mental problems on the needy archbishop. To just keep up with the parishes' needs in Chicago, Feehan quickly incardinated this mixed bag of clerics without having a real screening process in place. After all, they were all brother priests, right? This is where his most serious problem began.

Among the imported clergy, Irish-born priests of European training were known to be haughty, severe, and self-righteous—often influenced by a kind of Catholic Puritanism known as Jansenism. Jansenism, which was eventually condemned by the Church, was named after Cornelius Otto Jansen, a Flemish theologian and bishop of Ypres, Holland, in the early 1600s who took heed from Martin Luther's anxieties and fear of eternal damnation. In Jansenism, human nature was considered naturally corrupt—full of lust and greed and evil—and was in need of salvation through strict discipline and penitence. Its proponents believed Jesus was a severe and inscrutable Redeemer and God demanded spiritual perfection and should be feared. Many of Feehan's immigrant priests naturally began displaying this tyrannical and tenacious mind-set in their new parishes in Chicago. They were of a cold and rigid character that began teaching parishioners the fear of eternal damnation. They preached that the proper reception of Holy Communion required purification on the part of the recipient; numerous parishioners were inherently unworthy of receiving the sacrament of the Eucharist. These clerics ruled with a heavy hand and invulnerable superiority. They believed they had the right to micromanage every parishioner's life down to the last detail and would not tolerate the slightest affront to their own mode of thinking, which they felt emanated directly from the Almighty Himself. Eventually, the many self-righteous, Jansenist, Irish-born priests also saw themselves as an elite corps that had a strong influence on Chicago church life, on the clergy, and on seminary training. After all, the archbishop was a native Irishman as well.

Before he knew it, Feehan found himself surrounded by many Irish-born priests in positions of power in some of the most important parishes and institutions of Chicago. These priests ruled severely both in religious affairs and in their respective communities. The immigrant priests were using their power of the pulpit and the Roman collar both to advance themselves and to manipulate the political, social, and even economic conditions in their parishes. By the time Feehan realized what was happening, he was already deeply entrenched in a major internal problem—his incardinated Irish priests were looking to perpetuate the same severe tyranny in Chicago that they had enforced in Ireland. This was not what the archbishop had envisioned for Chicago.

During the time this problem was brewing, Muldoon worked closely with Feehan for nine years, during which time the archbishop relied more and more upon Peter. By now, Muldoon had matured and developed into an outstanding preacher, a committed educator, an active builder, and an excellent administrator. The one thing Muldoon had yet to accomplish was to head his own parish. In October 1895, Muldoon replaced Patrick D. Gill as pastor of the parish of Saint Charles Borromeo while retaining his full-time duties in the Archdiocesan Chancery Office. Muldoon's new goal was to develop Saint Charles Borromeo into an ideal parish community, much like Damen had done for the parish of Holy Family years before. Muldoon was to build a compound that could be a future model and standard for the rest of the archdiocese. Father Muldoon, now the second pastor of Saint Charles Borromeo, was charged with the monumental task of building a new Cathedral-like church, a convent, and a new school. The new buildings would replace the humble multiuse structure that the parish had outgrown. The formidable rectory that was built only four years before was too recent, large, and lavish to be torn down. That dense, three-story, fortresslike rectory built in the wake of the Great Chicago Fire and constructed of huge fire-resistant Indiana limestone blocks would be Father Gill's legacy to the parish.

Wisely, Pastor Muldoon built his ministry on the solid community put in place by his predecessor. Calling together his new congregation at nighttime meetings, Muldoon revealed his golden dream of a magnificent parish complex with nothing but empty prairie and swampland fanning out to the open west. The parish would be constructed in stages. The first building would be a glorious church, and after that, the new school and convent would be constructed. Needless to say, the response from parishioners was enthusiastic and overwhelmingly favorable. But these lofty dreams far exceeded the modest finances of the parish. By consensus, it was resolved to build the new church in two stages. At first, the basement would serve as the great meeting place and parish hall. It would be built with exterior stonework that

St. Charles Borromeo Church complex on the northwest corner of Roosevelt Road and Hoyne Avenue. (Reprinted from *Silver Jubilee: Saint Charles Borromeo: 1885–1910.*)

would take the edifice to the first floor. Then in phase two, the rest of the massive stone superstructure would be constructed.

The bold design of the new church was to stand taller than any other structure on Roosevelt Road—on a clear day,

The main altar of St. Charles Borromeo. (Reprinted from *Silver Jubilee: Saint Charles Borromeo: 1885–1910.*)

to be seen for miles. It would be a masterpiece of stone, glass, and wood, made of the finest materials known, each piece fashioned by skilled craftspeople and artisans. It was to be a holy building constructed to withstand the ravages of time and nature that would proclaim to the world at large the resurgence of an energized immigrant community bursting with pride and proclaiming architectural achievement for the greater glory of God, a true "Rock of Ages." Father Muldoon, along with the architect Martin Carr, envisioned a lofty and stately spire, crowned by a dazzling gold cross, whose soaring beauty would lift eyes up to the heavens. The laying of the cornerstone of the new Saint Charles Borromeo Church took place on July 26, 1896.

The new Saint Charles Borromeo complex would be welcoming and second to none in splendor in all Chicagoland. But, above all, this beautiful church was functional, designed to enhance and make liturgies like Masses, weddings, and funerals easier amid overwhelming beauty. Step by step, stone by stone, detail by detail, this new ecclesiastical form broke through the rich topsoil of the prairie. As the second phase of construction began to materialize, Muldoon turned his full attention to the heart of this lofty interior space, the exquisite main altar. It was a centerpiece of dazzling milky white marble with a background rising two stories and stone intricately carved like fine Irish lace, replete with ornate Gothic peaks, ancient symbols, flowers carved in marble, figures of saints and angels, all united in balanced harmony and beauty—like music set in stone. The main altar was designed as an eye-riveting feasting table for the Christian community for the ritual of the Mass. Ritual is the process through which people better understand the mysteries of life. Here, with this magnificent altar, they would be challenged and lifted to consider and reconsider the living gift of the Eucharist and the gift of a conscious afterlife in heaven.

During the time in which Muldoon was pastor of Saint Charles, the two mentors who greatly influenced his pastoral life, Father Coughlin and Archbishop Feehan, began to show their age. In the early 1890s, after years of pastoral service at Our Lady of Lourdes, Father Coughlin became so ill that he was forced to give up his pastorate. On leaving his parish, he traveled throughout the United States seeking a home with a milder climate where he could live a healthy retirement. After moving from place to place for a while, Father Coughlin eventually returned to Chicago. Well aware of his uncle's disabilities, the young then-pastor invited his mother's brother to serve with him as an assistant at Saint Charles until April 8, 1904. Father Coughlin accepted and

served in that capacity for many years. Giving his uncle a home in the lavish rectory was a small way for Muldoon to repay him for years of care and friendship and for the strong priestly example he set. Fittingly, on February 28, 1897, seven months after its cornerstone was laid on July 26, 1896,

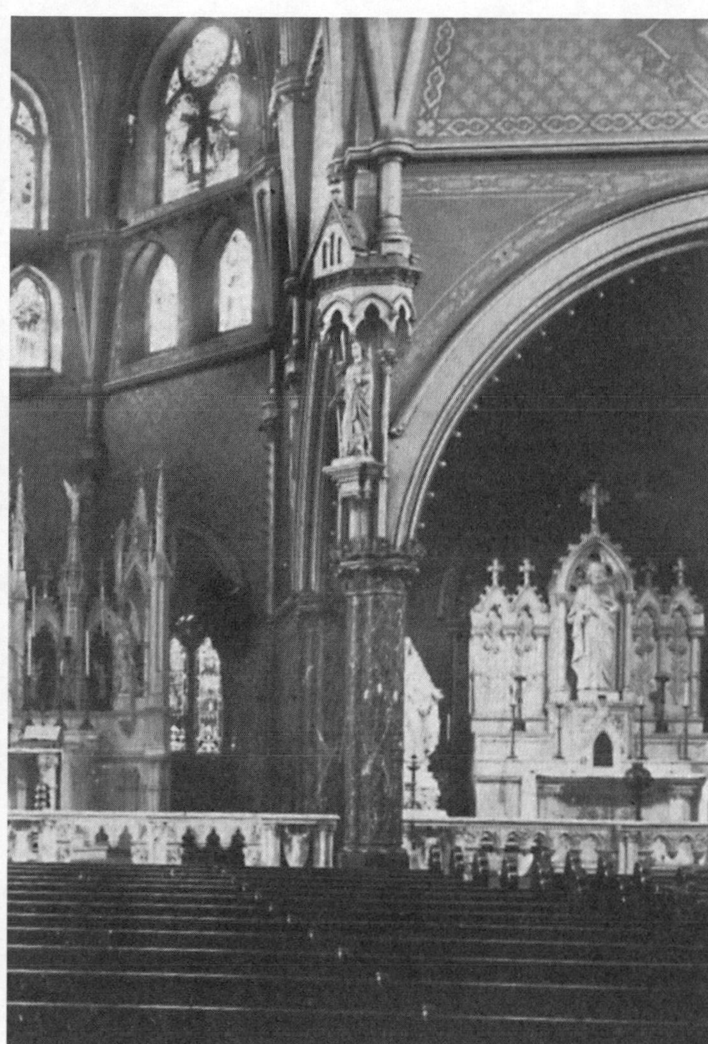

The sanctuary of St. Charles Borromeo. (Reprinted from *Silver Jubilee: Saint Charles Borromeo: 1885–1910.*)

Father John Coughlin was accorded the reciprocating privilege of celebrating the first Mass in the newly completed church at his nephew's new parish.

Also during this time, Feehan realized that the Catholic Church in Chicago should not be Irish through and through,

Pastor Peter J. Muldoon donated the east transept window depicting a scene in the life of St. Charles Borromeo. (Reprinted from *Silver Jubilee: Saint Charles Borromeo: 1885–1910.*)

so he began cultivating more priests from American seminaries as an alternative to having so many shipped over from Ireland. Archbishop Feehan began relying less and less upon the Irish-born clergy for leadership and focused more upon his American-born assistants and advisers, especially his secretary and chancellor. In 1895 Archbishop Feehan's health faltered, which was not surprising given his overwhelming workload. Overworked and aging, he petitioned the Holy See for needed help in his administrative and ceremonial duties, which were quite heavy considering the developing new parishes. Initially, Feehan selected Alexander J. McGavick, an American-born priest of Irish immigrant parents, as his first auxiliary. However, after he was consecrated, McGavick proved to be too ill to perform effective episcopal work, so Feehan had to select another auxiliary bishop. Feehan was determined to choose a man with whom he was familiar and knew would continue to build upon his legacy of work. His choice was a young American-born Irishman educated in an American seminary. This decision would spark a clerical firestorm that would not be quelled for a generation.

Feehan's first appointment as auxiliary bishop, Right Reverend A.J. McGavick, was too ill to maintain his position. (Reprinted from *Silver Jubilee: Saint Charles Borromeo: 1885–1910.*)

∞

Beyond the elaboration and elegance of the main altar of Saint Charles Borromeo Church, Muldoon had something else very special in mind. There was a walkway behind the altar that stretched about five or six feet wide to the back wall of the sanctuary, a path a bit larger than usual. Then, in the back wall of the altar, there was a marble panel that could readily be removed to reveal a hollow opening in the altar the size of a casket. In designing the majesty and functionality of the main altar, Muldoon also built it to be his mausoleum. With the additional room and some minor masonry work, the main altar could easily facilitate Muldoon's burial in the Church of Saint Charles Borromeo. With this in mind, many things make sense. In addition to his relationship with parishioners, Muldoon had a strong bond with the physical building of Saint Charles. His tie was so strong that he even envisioned his burial in the church he designed and built. Ghosts are known to haunt sites they were connected with while alive. Because Muldoon had invested so much time and effort in Saint Charles when he was alive, and perhaps because his remains never made it back to this intended resting place, it is no wonder that he came back to visit—to haunt—the place that he considered his home.

Chapter Twelve

Muldoon's Anguish

IT WAS LIKE LIGHTING THE WICK of a stick of dynamite. Initially, no one opposed the appointment of McGavick as the first auxiliary bishop of Chicago, but everyone took notice, especially the imported Irish clergy. Archbishop Feehan wasn't considering his "true" fellow countrymen for a significant position of influence and probable succession. He was looking to priests educated in American seminaries and born on American soil, who innately understood American culture. To be so readily overlooked, almost discriminated against, was insulting to the brotherhood of the Irish-born clergy. It was downright traitorous. So, in a matter of months, when the Illinois-born Father McGavick was forced to resign due to his own failing health, the window of opportunity opened once again for the Irish-born. Perhaps with some politicking and by putting pressure on the archbishop, the greenhorns could win back their stronghold in the Chicago system. They wanted an Irish-born priest to be selected as the new auxiliary bishop and needed to showcase a worthy candidate to Feehan. Their nomination was a young and hard-hitting luminary, Jeremiah J. Crowley, the Irish-born pastor of Saint Mary's in Oregon, Illinois. After all these quiet years in America, Crowley at last had a new cause to feed on.

Jeremiah J. Crowley was born on November 29, 1861, in the area of Colomane, Cork, Ireland, not far from the larger city of Bantry, and a scant year before the birth of the adversary he would come to hate in the future, Peter J. Muldoon. Not too much is known of Crowley's youth in Ireland. His father was a struggling farmer, working the rock-filled, unforgiving soil of a small plot of farmland at the farthest reaches of southwestern Ireland. He had at least one older brother, who was named John. Young Jeremiah never knew his mother, Nora Burke, except from ancient photographs. She died at his birth. Jeremiah's father marshaled all his sparse resources and sacrificed mightily to provide his young son with the opportunity he himself never had—a solid primary and secondary education. At great personal expense, he first sent his son to a boarding school, an option that was the prerogative of only the elite at that time. In 1876 he attended Saint Finbarr's College in Cork. By 1881 Jeremiah had sufficiently advanced himself and expressed his desire to become a Roman Catholic priest. He was sent to Saint Patrick's Seminary in County Carlow, where he completed his studies for the priesthood. At the age of 24, Jeremiah J. Crowley was ordained in Saint Patrick's Chapel by Bishop James Lynch for the diocese at County Cork on June 15, 1886, coincidentally the same year Muldoon was ordained in New York.

It was customary for many young Irish clerics, in a land of priestly surplus, to be sent to a foreign country for a short time for missionary service. Crowley's first assignment was in the United States at a parish in Manchester, New

Hampshire, where he served for two years. In September of 1888 he was sent to his first priestly assignment on Irish soil, as curate of Goleen. His parishioners were mainly poor farmworkers, many like his father, who labored on the ungenerous and exhausted soil set at the westernmost place in Cork, at the edge of the roaring sea. After two years of parish work, Crowley put on the mantle of reformer and dissenter. Prophetically, he took on the political system by becoming the lead figure in a land law case, coming to the aid of an elderly Protestant man being evicted by Protestant landlords. In this extremely unusual situation, in which a Roman Catholic priest came to the aid of a Protestant man being persecuted by his own church and the English government, Father Crowley began making a name for himself. He took the moral high ground of helping a poor old man down on his luck, now with nowhere to go. The case and the rebel-

The self-proclaimed "new Luther," Reverend Jeremiah J. Crowley. (Reprinted from *A Rebel with Many Causes.*)

lious Crowley received much notoriety, attracting the attention of people as far away as the distant capital of Dublin.

The charismatic Father Crowley enjoyed his newfound political voice along with the fame that came with it. Eventually, it seems, his popularity and reputation went straight to his head. Crowley thought of himself as indisputable, one whose own words about morality should be law. But they weren't. According to British rule at that time, outsiders were not to interfere with the matters between a tenant and a landlord. The local authorities also viewed Father Crowley as dangerous, ready and able to incite massive political unrest. The English establishment zeroed in on Crowley and hit him hard. He was served with three summonses for a trial that began on June 20, 1890, and lasted three days. Cecil Roche, the magistrate of Shull, a small city on the ocean where Crowley was called to trial, officially observed that Father Crowley had come to believe that anyone entering his political territory should bow down to his extreme personality. Because of the restless crowds surrounding the hearing, the trial was moved from Shull to Cork and delayed a week. Crowley was stunned when he was eventually sentenced to six months in prison for his opposition to the Crimes Act of 1887.

Once found guilty, Crowley was moved quickly and quietly by military troops to a prison in Cork. Half a year later when his prison term ended, Father Crowley, now an enemy of the state, was given 12 months probation with the stipulation that if he caused any further public unrest, he would be returned to prison for another six months—without trial. Clearly, the local government was nervous about the volatile priest who had the power to unleash a groundswell of opposition against authority. Because of his righteous stance against the English lords, Crowley was now muzzled. And he could not stand it. In addition to the government censure, the Catholic Church made it clear that Crowley needed to be put in his place and end his mutinous antics. After being reassigned to a parish in Newceston, Cork, Father Crowley, in the darkness of night and without anyone's knowledge, left his native Ireland for a new life and a new start where he had once served as a missionary, in the United States.

Once on American soil, Crowley returned to the parish in New Hampshire where he had served at the beginning of his ministry. But he was dissatisfied with Manchester. Crowley didn't see the opportunity for recognition in the New England town. He wanted bigger and better. Crowley then moved to New York City, where he was not accepted for incardination into the diocese. Later, during a massive Irish immigration, he moved to Chicago. There was no such thing as character analysis or an in-depth background check in Chicago, so when the needy Archbishop Feehan met Crowley, who was armed with letters of recommendation from local parishioners from his homeland, Crowley was readily accepted. Father Jeremiah J. Crowley was incardinated into the Chicago Archdiocese in 1896 and assigned as an assistant pastor to the Church of the Nativity of Our Lord at 37th Street and Union on Chicago's South Side, close to the famous Chicago stockyards, where many Irish Catholics worked. Crowley ministered to the needs of the parish for three years without incident. Then on December 12, 1899, he was appointed pastor of Saint Mary's parish in far-off Oregon, Illinois, a one-Catholic-Church town southwest of Rockford. For more than ten years, Crowley was dormant, like a bear in winter hibernation. However, time would show that he was unchanged from his militant days in Ireland. All he needed was a cause to stir him up and propel him to the forefront once again. The opportunity arose soon.

In 1900, not long after Crowley's move to Saint Mary's, Archbishop Feehan nominated the experienced Muldoon for the position of auxiliary bishop to replace the seriously ill Alexander McGavick, and Father Jeremiah Crowley was

St. Mary's Parish in Oregon, Illinois, was Father Crowley's pastoral residence during his push to succeed McGavick as Chicago's auxiliary bishop. (Photo by David Facchini and Marko Kevo.)

thrust into the spotlight as the dissenting party's leader and alternative—it's not really certain which came first. Before the archbishop knew it, he was in the middle of a civil war. It was the clique of prominent Irish-born priests against the rest of the archdiocese in a political battle for power. In the drama pitting brother priest against brother priest, the Irish-born clergy would pull out all the stops to solidify this position of prominence for Crowley. Soon after Muldoon was nominated to the episcopacy, a trio of prominent Irish-born

Chicago pastors—Thomas F. Cashman, Thomas P. Hodnett, and Hugh P. Smith—soon rallied together a tough and polarized coalition of 30 Irish-born priests to use what they called "legitimate and acceptable means" to derail Muldoon's appointment. They appealed directly to Archbishop Feehan, asking him to reconsider his nomination. Needless to say, Feehan maintained his prerogative and was unwavering in his support for his chancellor. Their appeal was ignored. Not to be easily defeated, the faction decided to go over the archbishop's head with a petition to the Vatican through the apostolic delegate, Sebastian Cardinal Martinelli (the Vatican's representative to the United States), and the mudslinging began. The letter accused Feehan of discriminating against Irish-born priests, maligned the reputation of Father Muldoon, and requested that the Pope himself would appoint Father Crowley as auxiliary bishop. This unconventional and drastic measure was overlooked by Rome. The Vatican decided that Feehan knew best about who should be appointed as his auxiliary. The appointment of Muldoon would stand.

Despite the demoralizing blow, Father Crowley and his supporters, who came to be known as Crowleyites, came out of their corner with fists swinging. In January 1901 a second letter was sent to Cardinal Martinelli, again pleading their case but also threatening to make their accusations public. The letter directly accused Bishop-elect Muldoon of gross immorality and implicated Bishop McGavick and nine other priests close to the archbishop in specific immoralities, including drunkenness, violating their vows of celibacy, and a list of other indictments such as abusing power and fiscal mismanagement. It was a low blow. Such damaging charges, especially if they were unfounded, were unheard of. Having them come from a group of fellow priests made the allegations much more serious, not to mention much more believable.

Through a series of strategic moves by the Irish-born priests, Father Crowley suddenly had a lot at stake. As leader of this dissenting group making such serious charges, Crowley's morality and reputation was on the line. He also had a lot to gain. With a coalition of Irish-born priests endorsing him, perhaps he could finally secure a position of power and make a name for himself once again. But it wasn't meant to be. Cardinal Martinelli dismissed all the charges and allowed for the appointment of Muldoon. The Crowleyites had failed once again.

At the end of his rope, the frustrated Crowley was tired of being ignored. It was time for something more dramatic. In a bitter protest, Father Crowley resigned his parish in Oregon. He would rather not serve at all than be a subordinate to Muldoon. It was the kind of drastic move that Crowley was famous for back in Ireland. Maybe he believed that this public act of dissent would incite an uprising or at least keep Archbishop Feehan from supporting Muldoon. But Feehan just accepted Crowley's resignation of his pastorate.

On Saturday, July 20, 1901, the *Chicago Daily Tribune* announced in bullet headlines: "Sebastian Cardinal Martinelli comes to Consecrate. Martinelli Comes to Chicago and Father Muldoon will soon be a Bishop." This extraordinary step signified the Holy Father's full approval of Muldoon. Instead of being consecrated by a local prelate, the Vatican's apostolic delegate to the United States would preside over the ritual himself. It was a diplomatic slap in the face to Crowley and the Irish-born faction. The *Chicago Daily Tribune* article quotes Cardinal Martinelli as follows:

> "Well, Rome does not seem wrought up about it anyway," resumed the prelate. "If any protest against Father Muldoon was sent to the Holy See, it was dis-

> posed there as groundless. Had it been recognized there as valid, the arraignment would have been sent to me for an investigation. All I know is that the bulls appointing Father Muldoon Auxiliary Bishop were signed by the Holy Father on July 11, and that ceremony having been ordered by the Pontiff, nothing now can stop it. I propose to consecrate Father Muldoon next week according to plan."

∞

Times have not changed. The same remains true today. A priest's most vulnerable points are his sense of morality and his vow of celibacy. Once that reputation is tarnished, full recovery is virtually impossible. Even if the accused priest is exonerated of all charges and the accusations against him are unfounded, there will always remain some doubt in the public mind. The priest will be watched more carefully. People will wonder if there was a cover-up or if the truth was really revealed. In light of recent church scandals regarding pedophilia and sexual aberrations, these accusations against Muldoon seem quite tame. But in the simpler days of the early twentieth century, charges of corruption were, for the most part, unthinkable. The public infighting and charges were so extraordinary, the Crowley scandal made national headlines and became an international incident.

So the big question is, Were these accusations against Muldoon true or false? When the Irish-born priests were asked to publicly provide detailed accounts of the immoralities they charged against Muldoon, they remained silent. On July 19, 1901, the Chicago Daily Tribune wrote, "Since it became apparent that the Pope had considered the charges groundless, the priests who signed the protest against Father Muldoon have been reticent about stating the nature of their plaint. The Rev. T.P. Hodnett, Pastor of the Church of the

Immaculate Conception, was one of the prime movers in the opposition but he refused to state the contents of the formal charges beyond the fact that they were 'extremely grave'." Father Muldoon was later quoted in that same article as saying, "I know nothing about this dissention. Whatever the charges are, I know they are false and since the Holy See has seen fit to ignore them I can afford to smile at my enemies." In the eyes of the Church, Muldoon was absolutely clean of the vilest case of false witness in Chicago church history to that time—charges so foul that they tarnished Muldoon's reputation for the rest of his lifetime. Maybe even longer.

Chapter Thirteen

Cathedral Under Siege

BY NOW NO ONE KNEW WHAT TO think of the vague public charges brought up by the Crowleyites. Muldoon tried to dismiss the accusations and was quoted as saying, "The cause of the schism is that I am an American. It is the old story of the Irish priests against the Americans." While he tried to defuse the situation and salvage his reputation, Crowley hit back harder with subtle threats. "I do not feel at liberty to say what action we have resolved on . . . but it will become public all in good time."

Frank McGrath shared with me the following family story about his mother's sister, Kate: The Scanlons were parishioners of Saint Charles Borromeo parish. During the days prior to Muldoon's episcopal ordination, young Catherine Scanlon, somewhere in her early teens, was riding a streetcar home. On her ride, she overheard a couple of men plotting to kill the soon-to-be-consecrated Bishop Muldoon. With that, the young girl immediately jumped

Holy Name Cathedral became the setting for a showdown between Muldoon and Crowley on July 21, 1901. (Reprinted from *Souvenir of the Archdiocese of Chicago, Commemorating the Installation of the Most Reverend George W. Mundelein, D.D. February 19, 1916.*)

from the trolley and ran home to tell her parents, who then warned Father Muldoon and the powers that be. This is not the only account of Muldoon being a hunted man. On Monday, July 22, 1901, the *Tribune* declared, "Fight Muldoon in a Placard. Men drive about the city at night posting circulars near the Catholic Churches. Police are after them. Reference made to alleged resignation of Father Crowley and charges credited to it. Father Barry (rector of Holy Name Cathedral) declares perpetrator of an assassin." The distributed placard read, "The Consecration of Father Muldoon on Thursday will be the blasphemy of the twentieth century. Watch for Father Crowley's letter of resignation." It was apparent that Crowley was a man of drastic means, and no one was quite sure how far he would go.

As the day of consecration approached, it was too dangerous for Muldoon to appear on the street alone. The threat of being murdered was too great. The young Bishop-elect's parishioners from Saint Charles and members of various Catholic societies served as his round-the-clock bodyguards, serving as a human shield whenever he appeared in public. These diligent protectors blanketed his rectory, the chancery, and even Holy Name Cathedral on the day of his consecration. Unfortunately, at a time when Muldoon should have been preparing for a jubilant celebration and a career milestone, he now feared for his life as the attack against his reputation continued. Two days before the ceremony, the following letter from Crowley was published in the *Chicago Record-Herald:*

> Most-Reverend Sir:
>
> I . . . herby protest the appointment of your nominee, Rev. Father P.J. Muldoon for auxiliary bishop of Chicago. The reasons have already been forwarded to Rome, but I have a moral certainty that they were intercepted or purloined, because if the holy

> see were in possession of the very grave charges, Muldoon's appointment would never have been sanctioned. . . .
>
> Those men you champion, though of Irish descent and of undeniable Irish names, are also known to you for having unreasonable and fierce antipathy to the people and the priests of that nationality in particular and to those of foreign birth in general. They referred to them as "Micks" and "Biddies," "Frog-eaters," "Dagoes," "Polacks" and "German Plugs," and on every occasion are discriminated against, though they are indebted for their education to these generous loyal Catholic people. In a word, with your knowledge they are using language and pursuing methods that are calculated to the absolute disintegration of your archdiocese.
>
> And you are now going to cap the climax by making their leader and boon companion P.J. Muldoon a bishop of the holy Catholic church? For twenty years you have ignored the intelligent, influential and loyal Catholics of your diocese. You gave them no recognition whatsoever, save as sources of revenue. You habitually spoke of them with contempt and strenuously opposed every suggestion that pointed toward their recognition. Hence, to-day it is universally recognized both by the laity and clergy that your archdiocese is in a state of chaos and that all ecclesiastical discipline is broken.

Envision the Holy Name Cathedral at Chicago Avenue and State Street as the potential battleground for the Cain and Abel of 1901. It was the day of consecration. Public access was restricted and admission was mainly by invitation only. Guards were stationed at each door, ready to

Interior of Holy Name Cathedral. (Reprinted from *Souvenir of the Archdiocese of Chicago, Commemorating the Installation of the Most Reverend George W. Mundelein, D.D. February 19, 1916.*)

thwart any assassination attempt or disturbance by the Crowleyites. But it never was needed. Peter J. Muldoon was consecrated as auxiliary bishop to Archbishop Patrick A. Feehan in Chicago's Holy Name Cathedral on July 25, 1901. Crowley and his group did not show themselves on that day. After his consecration, the new bishop was taken by horse and carriage in a large procession to the corner of Ashland

Avenue and Jackson Boulevard, on the city's West Side. A massive crowd from Saint Charles Borromeo parish assembled there, carrying brilliant banners and lighted candles to congratulate their newly consecrated pastor.

Following Muldoon's consecration, Cardinal Martinelli commanded that the priests of the Irish-born insurgency desist or be suspended, and he demanded that Father Crowley submit to Archbishop Feehan or be excommunicated. These were serious instructions. It was clear that the Irish-born had lost this battle and would lose a lot more if they continued with the war. Everything that these priests had worked for within their respective parishes and within the diocese—prestige, income, relationships—would be taken away, perhaps permanently, if they continued their protest against Muldoon. The Irish-born knew that their leadership positions within the community depended on the Roman collar they wore. If that was stripped from them, all would be lost. There was no choice but to make amends.

Archbishop Feehan extended a healing hand to the Crowleyites by allowing them to retain their positions without interruption in exchange for a renewed brotherhood that included all the priests in the archdiocese, regardless of where they were born. With that, the open conflict ceased, though much of it went underground. Slowly, and in many cases begrudgingly, the Irish-born capitulated to Archbishop Feehan, and it was business as usual. Except for Crowley. Literally a leader with no followers, Father Crowley was in the deepest trouble of them all. Since Crowley had already resigned his parish, Martinelli decided that if Crowley still refused to repent for the damage he had caused, he would be excommunicated. Soon after Muldoon's consecration, Crowley scheduled an appointment with Archbishop Feehan to resentfully make amends. It wouldn't be that easy for him. On the day Father Crowley arrived at the archbishop's residence, Feehan was nowhere to be found. Instead, Feehan had arranged for the rebellious priest to submit his apology and request for reinstatement directly to Bishop Muldoon. Crowley would have none of that! He refused to speak to anyone else that day, especially Muldoon. He waited all day in the waiting room at the archbishop's residence, refusing to leave without speaking with Feehan, who never arrived for the meeting. Eventually, Crowley had to be removed by the Chicago police.

Defiant and stubborn as ever, Crowley decided that he would return to Oregon, Illinois, to claim his parish without apologizing to the archdiocese through Bishop Muldoon. But Feehan was a step ahead of him. The archbishop had already notified the local municipality that Father Crowley was not allowed to enter Saint Mary's. When Crowley tried to take over his parish by force, sheriffs working under a court order removed him. This activity led to legal action. Crowley took his case against Archbishop Feehan to the Illinois Courthouse in Freeport, Illinois, to have his injunction dissolved. Crowley lost his case against Feehan, losing his parish, church, and rectory. With his pride standing in the way, Crowley had lost it all, was alone, and had nowhere to go.

By October, Crowley turned on his Church completely. It had been four months since Muldoon's consecration, and the defiant-as-ever Crowley continued to publicly attack Muldoon and other prominent clerics as evil corrupters of the teachings of Christ. Enough was enough, and Cardinal Martinelli stepped back into the picture to enforce his threat. Crowley was publicly excommunicated, considered *vitandus* (to be avoided). On October 25, 1901, the *Chicago Daily Tribune* reported: "[The] Deposed Man [Crowley] Now Declared To Be Dead . . . so far as the local authorities are concerned in this matter [excommunication]." And dead he was to the Catholic faithful of the Chicago Archdiocese. A decree was posted in every archdiocesan sacristy for 30

Peter J. Muldoon on the day of his consecration as Auxiliary Bishop of the Archdiocese of Chicago, July 25, 1901. (Reprinted from *That All May Be One: The History of the Rockford Diocese.*)

days, saying that Crowley was an outlaw of Catholicism. Though recognized by people everywhere in Chicago due to the scandal, Crowley was totally ignored. He was treated as if he had never existed. The penalty was so severe that should he walk into a church service, the rite would be halted immediately. This happened at least twice, once at Old Saint Peter's Church at Clark and Polk. Then again, in a striking show of defiance, Crowley paraded down the main aisle of Holy Name Cathedral before a full congregation, knowingly stopping the liturgy. Whispers erupted from the awed parishioners. Candles were swiftly extinguished, the choir left its position, and the celebrant, Monsignor Barry, climbed the pulpit. Pointing his finger at Crowley, the rector of Holy Name publicly excoriated and humiliated the excommunicated priest. Afterward, the congregation completely cleared out of the church until Crowley was left all by himself to eventually be evicted by the police.

∞

On July 25, 1901, the Chicago Daily Tribune wrote about the great welcome for Muldoon on the evening of his consecration as bishop:

> Bishop Muldoon started home, escorted by 200 members of Catholic societies, shortly before 8 o'clock. He rode in a closed carriage and was accompanied by Father Kearney, Father Barth, and Vicar-General Fitzsimmons. When the Bishop arrived at Ashland and Jackson Boulevards, he was met by a procession, which had marched from Saint Charles Parish; from that point those in the parade escorted the new bishop to his home.
>
> Thousands of persons lined the sidewalk and cheered. At the street intersections, it was almost impossible for the escort to clear the way for the

party. As the new Bishop arrived in front of his home, a blaze of electric lights flashed from its front forming, in Latin, the words, "Behold, Our Great Priest." As the lights flashed, the thousands of persons massed around the house set up a cheer, which lasted until Bishop Muldoon had stepped from his carriage, when he was showered with floral pieces.

"This sincere welcome draws only words of appreciation from me", spoke Bishop Muldoon, as he faced his friends. "But tonight the words nearest to my heart are 'Home, Sweet Home.' Be it ever so humble, it will always be dear to me. A far deeper motive than a mere welcome to me personally inspires this tonight. You have a Catholic reverence for the office for which I have been called to fill. It shows when Rome speaks, the spirit of loyalty and obedience is uppermost."

Chapter Fourteen

A Bitter Harvest

SIX DAYS AFTER HIS EPISCOPAL consecration, Bishop Muldoon was appointed vicar general of the Archdiocese of Chicago, officially second in command after Feehan. Almost immediately, Muldoon assisted the aging Feehan with the stockpiled work of the archdiocese—confirmations, dedications of churches and schools, laying cornerstones—taking an active part in the many ecclesiastical ceremonies required of a bishop. All the while, strength and energy slowly drained from the frail Archbishop Feehan, who increased his dependence on the young Muldoon. Feehan—a scholar, a gardener, and a prayerful man—spent quiet hours in theological thought or tending to his flower garden while Bishop Muldoon carried on with the heavier work in the archdiocese. Feehan did not last long in his infirmity, dying of an apoplectic stroke on July 12, 1902, about a year after Muldoon's consecration. Feehan was 73.

Muldoon deeply grieved the death of Feehan, who was his spiritual leader, mentor, and confidant. After Feehan's death, Muldoon was appointed administrator of the archdiocese. Most people naturally assumed that Muldoon was going to be Chicago's next archbishop, maybe even a cardinal. He was the odds-on favorite. The process of finding a new archbishop, however, is more complex than that. Three names were submitted to Rome on a document called a *terna* (a list of three). One of the nominees was to be selected as Chicago's next archbishop. Bishop Muldoon was nominated along with two others from Illinois, Bishop John Lancaster Spalding of Peoria and Bishop James Ryan of Alton. Bishop Spalding quickly withdrew himself from contention when his estranged lover threatened to publicly expose her sexual relationship with him. This left two candidates in the running, and both were passed over. Out of the blue, the Vatican appointed a dark horse, Bishop James Edward Quigley of Buffalo, New York, as archbishop to Chicago on January 8, 1903. Archbishop Quigley was installed on June 12, 1903.

Shortly after his excommunication, Crowley remarkably was given a chance for a fresh start. Toward the end of 1901, Bishop Richard Scannel of Omaha, Nebraska, saw to lifting the ban of his Chicago excommunication. Somehow, Crowley had convinced someone into quietly reinstating him into the Church. Surprisingly, there is no record of either Archbishop Feehan or Bishop Muldoon objecting to his reinstatement. Perhaps they were both tired of dealing with Crowley and his antics, and Feehan's failing health probably kept both priests focused on bigger issues facing the archdiocese. Father Crowley took a six-month leave of absence before actively becoming a priest again. Rumor had it that he even celebrated Mass at Holy Name Cathedral.

Less than two years after the death of Archbishop Feehan, Muldoon suffered another personal tragedy. Father John Coughlin, Muldoon's uncle and lifelong friend, died on April 4, 1904. His funeral Mass took place at Saint Charles

Most Reverend James E. Quigley, successor to Archbishop Feehan. (Reprinted from *Diamond Jubilee of the Archdiocese of Chicago, 1920.*)

Borromeo, where he had last served as an assistant to his nephew. After the final services in the church that Muldoon had built, Father Coughlin's remains were transported to Providence, Rhode Island, to be interred with the deceased of the Muldoon family. Sadly, within three years of his consecration, Bishop Muldoon had lost the two greatest role models in his life.

Most notably in his career, Bishop Muldoon worked hand in hand with the two most prolific brick-and-mortar archbishops in the history of Chicago. Next to Feehan, who was responsible for erecting 140 structures, Quigley constructed 113 new churches between 1903 and 1915. Muldoon served him as vicar general from 1903 until 1908. At the suggestion of Archbishop Quigley, a new Diocese of Rockford, Illinois, was established in 1908 with Peter J. Muldoon as its first and founding bishop. His days at Saint Charles were over. Muldoon suddenly realized that he would no longer live in the same company of the people who had rallied to his defense during the vitriolic and traumatic Crowley days. No longer would he regularly celebrate Mass in the grand edifice he helped design and create. His total commitment was now to Rockford, the new diocese that oversaw Crowley's former parish in Oregon, Illinois.

The following excerpts from Muldoon's farewell to Saint Charles are taken from the parish Jubilee Book of 1910:

> December 13, [1908] the parish farewell to the pastor. A monster meeting was held in the parish hall. The whole demonstration was distinctly a parish affair. A program of songs, recitations and instrumental music by parishioners was followed by addresses by the assistant pastors, trustees of the church and presentation of a testimonial to the pastor, and a response by the Bishop.
>
> December 14, reception and farewell meeting to Rt. Rev. P.J. Muldoon at the Chicago Auditorium. Every seat in the auditorium was filled. Archbishop Quigley was chairman of the meeting. Mr. Thomas H. Cannon spoke on behalf of the Catholic Order of Foresters. Mr. James Maher gave an address in the name of the Knights of Columbus. Rev. E.A. Kelly spoke as representative of the clergy of the Archdiocese of Chicago. Special music arranged for the occasion was sung by a chorus of three hundred voices from the Catholic Order of Forester's Choral Society, under the direction of Mr. William F. Ryan. Mr. John P. Hopkins presented Bishop Peter J. Muldoon with a purse of $35,000 on behalf of the clergy and citizens of Chicago. Archbishop Quigley delivered an address and Bishop Muldoon spoke at the close of the meeting.
>
> December 15, Rt. Rev. Peter J. Muldoon left Chicago by special train, accompanied by two hundred clergymen, and about four hundred citizens.

When Muldoon departed Chicago, he left behind a dense industrial city, crowded with uncounted immigrants from every place on the face of the earth, for a rich and sparsely settled agricultural territory bounded on the west by the Mississippi River. At his coming, there were two Catholic churches in the city of Rockford. The new diocese numbered a Catholic population of 50,000 people and 74 priests as compared to Chicago's 1,150,000 Catholics and 685 priests. At the time the Rockford Diocese was founded, the rapidly growing American Catholic Church was becoming less and less of a missionary institution.

Muldoon plunged himself into the new role as ordinary of his new diocese. He showed himself as strong and as tireless in his work as he had been in Chicago. Again, he took on the role of a brick-and-mortar priest, constructing new parishes, churches, orphanages, facilities for the mentally ill, and homes for the aged that had never before existed in this territory. Bishop Muldoon became especially active in developing a system in Rockford using Chicago as a model. Much like Chicago, the composition of Catholics in Rockford was predominantly a combination of immigrant populations. As he learned from Archbishop Feehan, Muldoon was anxious to preserve the customs and practices of each different ethnic identity. He placed newcomers under the care of priests from their own countries so that new parishes were established for Poles, Ukrainians, Italians, and other smaller national groups, preserving their cultures and customs. His second concern was for widespread Catholic education. Even though Muldoon himself had attended public grammar and high schools in California, the new Rockford bishop focused his efforts on making a parochial education available to young Catholics.

From the day of Muldoon's consecration and further work in Chicago and Rockford, Father Crowley dedicated himself to destroying the reputation of Muldoon and the Roman Catholic Church. During the next seven years he would write three mean-spirited books printed by his own Menace Publishing Company. In 1905 Crowley wrote a 704-page book titled *The Parochial School: A Curse to the Church, a Menace to the Nation*, which attacked the Catholic school system, something that Muldoon had invested much time and effort in developing. In 1908, the same year that Muldoon became the head of the Rockford Diocese, Crowley resigned from the priesthood to undertake his own campaign of morality, billing himself as "the New Martin Luther." He later wrote these words of himself:

> In 1908, I voluntarily withdrew from the priesthood and the Roman Catholic Church. This step enabled me to say things which I could not say with propriety during my priesthood and while acting as a mere reformer within the Church.

In 1912 the bitter Crowley wrote the following in his second book, *Romanism, a Menace to the Nation*:

> [I]f the Government of the United States had done its plain duty in protecting my rights and interests as an American citizen during the past ten years, Cardinals Martinelli and Falconio, Archbishop Quigley, Bishop Muldoon, and many other Roman ecclesiastics would now be wearing stripes in penitentiaries as the guests of Uncle Sam, instead of purple and gold in luxurious palaces as "Ambassadors of Christ."

Later that same year, an angry mob in the small rural town of Oelwein, Iowa, attacked Crowley before he had the opportunity to present an anti-Catholic lecture. It was reported that the six-foot three-inch Crowley was nearly beaten to death. In 1913 Crowley wrote what was considered his masterpiece, *The Pope: Chief of White Slavers, High Priest of Intrigue.* The distribution of that book landed Crowley in two federal court cases where the Menace Publishing Company was brought up on charges of distributing pornographic material through the mail. As plaintiff, the federal government lost both cases.

On July 10, 1915, Archbishop Quigley died rather unexpectedly, leaving the leadership of the Chicago Archdiocese open once again. The popular yet controversial Bishop Muldoon was again nominated for the position. Jack Greeley passes on the legend that a senior Irish pastor announced the appointment of Chicago's new archbishop in the following manner: "M-u-n-d-e-l-e-i-n: That's one hell of a way to spell Muldoon!" George William Mundelein, auxiliary bishop of Brooklyn, New York, became Chicago's next archbishop, on December 9, 1915. He later became Chicago's first

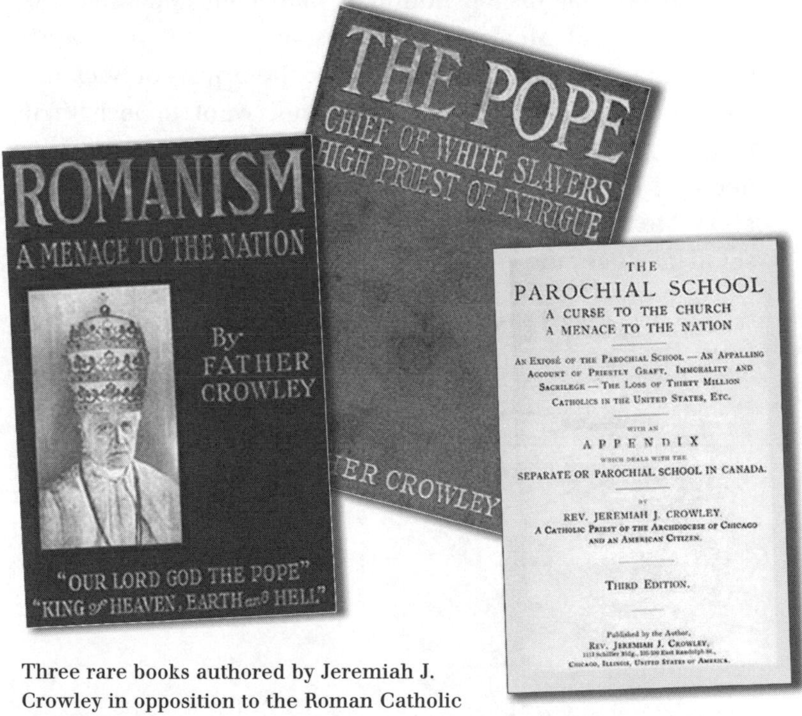

Three rare books authored by Jeremiah J. Crowley in opposition to the Roman Catholic Church. (Reprinted from www.redemptorist.org.)

cardinal, on March 24, 1924. He was the first cardinal created west of the Allegheny Mountains.

Bishop Muldoon went on to faithfully serve the Rockford Diocese for 19 years. During that time, he became a beloved leader of the Catholic community in Rockford. After being passed over once again to be archbishop of Chicago, Muldoon, at the suggestion of Cardinal Mundelein, the Vatican offered Muldoon the rural Diocese of Monterey, Los Angeles, back in his native state of California, where he could hopefully escape Crowley's damaging propaganda. Although this was the opportunity Muldoon had waited for his entire lifetime, the threat of American Indians in the "Wild West" at that time was a major deterrent. After five months of contemplation over the offer, Muldoon decided to accept the position. On March 22, 1917, the Associated Press announced that Bishop Muldoon had been appointed the new Bishop of Monterey and Los Angeles in his native California. But on hearing this news, the priests of Rockford were deeply distressed. They did not want to lose their leader, whom they had now come to love and respect so deeply. The Rockford clergy petitioned Pope Benedict XV to allow Muldoon to remain in Rockford. Bishop Muldoon was set to take over the West Coast Diocese in June of 1917, until

Chicago's first Cardinal, George Cardinal Mundelein, successor to Archbishop Quigley. (Reprinted from *Diamond Jubilee of the Archdiocese of Chicago, 1920.*)

he petitioned the Holy Father to allow him to remain in Rockford. The Pope, in a rare decision, reversed his appointment. To the great joy of the priests and people of Rockford, and by the independent decision of Muldoon, the bishop was allowed to remain in the diocese that he had fathered and founded.

Between 1917 and 1918, Muldoon would once again be thrown into the spotlight, becoming nationally known for his work in the war effort and for being a leader in social reform. He became a Catholic statesman for the nation by chairing the National Catholic War Council (now known as the United States Conference of Catholic Bishops) during World War I.

As Muldoon approached his 60s, his health began to weaken. While in Saint Louis, Missouri, on June 28, 1926, for the consecration of its new cathedral, Muldoon suddenly suffered from appendicitis, which, at that time, was a serious medical problem. After surgery, Muldoon spent nearly an entire year in recovery in Saint Louis at Saint John's Hospital. He was separated from the active work in his diocese until March 27, 1927, when he was allowed to return to Illinois. But Muldoon never recovered. The bedridden bishop died in Rockford on October 8, 1927. He was two days short of his 65th birthday. As it is common practice for a bishop to be buried in the diocese he last serves, burial in the crypt in the main altar of Saint Charles Borromeo was not even considered. Muldoon was interred at Saint Mary's Cemetery, just steps away from the Diocesan Chancery Office of Rockford.

Not much is known of what actually happened to Jeremiah J. Crowley. The last known report of him in the press (in the *New York Times* on September 13, 1913) was about his third book. After that, Crowley faded into oblivion. The records prior to 1901 regarding Saint Mary's Church in Oregon, Illinois, were destroyed in a fire at the parish; his personal writings were also lost in the blaze. The Rockford

Memorial dedicated to Bishop Muldoon in the Bishops' conference room of the N.C.W.C. Building, Washington, D.C. (Reprinted from *That All May Be One: The History of the Rockford Diocese.*)

Diocesan Anniversary Book of 1976 conveniently glosses over his tumultuous tenure in a mere sentence: "Father McCann was succeeded by Father Jeremiah J. Crowley, who in turn was followed by Father John S. Finn." It is rumored that the Diocesan Chancery Office of Rockford burned as many of Crowley's books as they could. Today, books from the Menace Publishing Company are rare collectors items, unavailable at most libraries.

As for his death, there are popular anti-Catholic theories that Pope Pius X ordered Father Crowley's assassination and that his body was secretly discarded. By popular Chicago legend, Father Crowley died a pauper in 1922. Supposedly, nurses who lived in the West Side hospital district, within Saint Jarlath's parish, reported to their pastor, Monsignor Thomas B. O'Brien, that an excommunicated Catholic priest was dying in nearby Cook County Hospital. By one account, I have heard that by the time that Monsignor O'Brien arrived to give Crowley the last rites, he was already dead. In another version of the story, Monsignor O'Brien identified the former priest, who was defiant to the very end. When Crowley was asked if he had anything to atone for, he refused to repent. Accordingly, the sad story relates that Monsignor O'Brien refused the dying man the final absolution of the Catholic Church. To this day, the exact whereabouts of Father Jeremiah J. Crowley's final resting place are unknown.

∞

The strong Irish presence in the Archdiocese of Chicago continues to this day, though the public infighting has long been extinguished. In The Irish in Chicago, it is documented that "Quigley and his successors accepted no more diocesan clergymen from Ireland into the Chicago Archdiocese, though a few immigrant Irish priests continued to wield influence in Chicago parishes well into the 1950's."

Ironically enough, the longest lasting of the Irish-born priests that Feehan imported was Monsignor O'Brien, the priest rumored to have refused last rites to Crowley. A reporter from the Chicago Daily News once interviewed O'Brien during his later years, to gain a firsthand, inside perspective from one of the last living survivors of the Crowley scandal. Soon after the interview began, O'Brien raised his hand, stopped the questioning, and said that "it was better to let sleeping dogs lie." Monsignor O'Brien died April 23, 1971, at the age of 93.

The legacy of both Crowley and Muldoon live on to this day. Some of my information about the life of Jeremiah J. Crowley was obtained from www.reformation.org, which lauds Father Crowley for his stance against Catholicism. I am sure that some Protestants do see Crowley as the Martin Luther of America.

While it is certain that the Crowley years stunted his growth, at least in Chicago, Bishop Muldoon nevertheless went on to be successful in his remaining priestly life. He was a luminary with the potential to become Chicago's first cardinal. Though nominated for archbishop twice and considered the

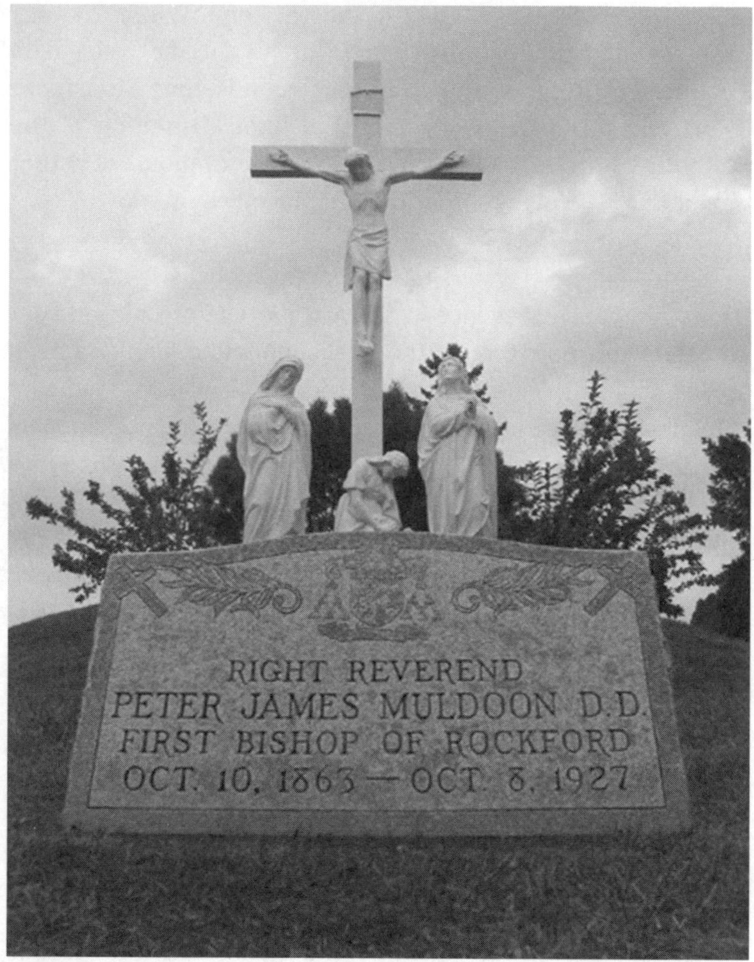

The grave site of Rockford's first bishop located in St. Mary's Cemetery in Rockford, Illinois. (Photo by David Facchini and Marko Kevo.)

front-runner both times, with a wounded public reputation that could not be overcome, Muldoon was overlooked. Today, his legacy silently lives on, through the U.S. Council of Catholic Bishops, through the diocese he founded in Rockford, and through the many churches that he helped Archbishops Feehan and Quigley erect in Chicago during that great, unparalleled time of expansion

Chapter Fifteen

Groaning from the Attic

THE EARLIEST GHOST STORIES begin shortly after Bishop Muldoon's death in Rockford in 1927. Assistant priests living in the rectory started noticing loud and disturbing noises seeping down from the third floor, which was primarily being used for storage by this time. Late at night, priests of the house woke to sounds of long groaning and deep whimpering coming from upstairs, as if someone were being slowly tortured on the third floor. Other times, there were sounds of banging and pounding coming from rooms where no one was staying, as if someone were locked in upstairs and trying to escape. The priests of the house eventually connected the racket coming from the third floor to Muldoon, revisiting his old chancery on Cypress. And so, the legend began.

One of the priests to experience the loud moaning in the rectory was Monsignor Matthew "Fritz" Canning, who was pastor of Saint Charles Borromeo during the years of

Prohibition and the Great Depression shortly after Muldoon's death. Fritz was working at Saint Charles with two assistants, all three of them ordained into the Minor Order of Exorcist (which was common for priests until 1972). Neither of the assistants in the house would volunteer to investigate the troubling nocturnal noises. The priests were very much afraid that the attic sounds were diabolical. The assistants were too intimidated to use the power of exorcism, but Pastor Canning was not. Armed with a purple stole, the *Rituale Romanum*, holy water, and a flashlight, Pastor Canning slowly ascended the dimly lit stairway alone to the rooms that seemed to be the source of the nighttime cacophony of noises. It was very quiet as Pastor Canning worked his way from room to room, meticulously investigating everything—the locked rooms packed with musty old books left behind by former pastors and assistants, as well as worn altar vestments in all of the colors of the liturgical calendar. As the priest ran across a wardrobe of hanging cassocks and aged black clerical suits, he made an unusual discovery. Moving his hand over one of the pockets of a dusty, moth-ridden black suit jacket, Pastor Canning felt a hard bulge in the right-hand side pocket. He felt around and pulled out a pyx, a vessel shaped like a pocket watch that was gold on the inside and used by priests to carry consecrated hosts for Communion to the sick and the elderly. To his consternation, as he opened the lid he found six yellowed consecrated hosts. He couldn't tell how long they had been there or how they had been forgotten in that suit, for that matter. To the Catholic, the consecrated host is God's great gift to humanity—the Body of Christ in the appearance of bread. Unused, consecrated hosts are kept in the church tabernacle, and it is the priests' thoughtful duty to make sure that the Body of Christ is stored there until it is properly consumed. It seemed that a priest of former days must have been on Communion calls while carrying the hosts to sick parishioners and forgot to remove the pyx from his pocket. Quite strange.

Pastor Canning immediately took the pyx with its precious contents into the priests' sacristy in the church, where he dissolved the aged hosts in a small bowl of tepid water. When the hosts had dissolved and were no longer bread, he poured the musty liquid into the sacrarium, a small porcelain sink bowl without faucets that fed into the ground, well below the church, for the respectful disposal of sacred objects. With the removal of the pyx of consecrated hosts, everyone in the rectory noticed that the nocturnal noises stopped at once. Peace had once again been restored to the rectory.

Monsignor Canning was an aggressive and daring leader who was good for the parish of Saint Charles. He was known to reach out to the dispossessed, most of whom had not been served by any of the other pastors after Muldoon. During the hard economic times of his tenure, the parish of Saint Charles began to change. As the longtime Irish moved out to the west, Italians replaced them on Taylor Street west of Ashland to Western Avenue. Having already served for a decade, Fritz realized it was time for a new appointment. Luckily, Pastor Canning went up to the third floor of the rectory and discovered an untouched room that Muldoon had once used as an office. There, left in the dust, were various papers never properly returned to the chancery, along with dusty old newspapers that detailed the public battles between Muldoon and Father Crowley. Canning called the chancery and said, "I think I have something I know you want. . . . the Crowley papers." Having had his fill of Saint Charles, the cunning pastor said, "They are yours in exchange for another assignment." Supposedly, this is how Monsignor Canning moved to Saint Ferdinand parish on the city's developing Northwest Side, where he eventually built a new church and remained there until he died.

∞

People have always been fascinated by the topic of exorcism—the religious rite of casting out the devil. In both ancient and modern history, there are many facts that point to the reality of diabolical possession. The ritual of exorcism can be traced back to the long and elaborate rite that Jews performed in the Old Testament. Violent and uncontrollable devils invaded people to be used as vessels to carry out anger and evil. In Luke 11:14–15, Jesus conducts one of many exorcisms, which He performs effortlessly. Through this passage, it is clear that Jesus was a man of power—and strength. This was evident not only in His teachings but also through the fact that demons feared Christ and obeyed His command. Before His ascension into heaven, Jesus' final charge to His disciples was to teach His Gospel to all nations and to drive out evil spirits. And so it has been the practice of the Roman Catholic Church, to ordain and commission priests with the power of Christ to cast out evil spirits.

In 1972 a watershed event took place. Prior to that, candidates for the priesthood received from their bishop the four minor orders of porter, lector, exorcist, and acolyte. The minor orders would then be followed by the major orders of subdeacon, deacon, and priest. Under the new reform, the orders of porter, exorcist, and subdeacon were eliminated. Since then, not every priest is ordained with the power to act as an exorcist. Today the head of the diocese or archdiocese selects which priests will become exorcists. That decision is still made according to provisions of the Rituale Romanum, issued under the authority of Pope Paul V, June 17, 1614, where an exorcist is selected by the clear virtue and probity of his life, among other moral qualifications. Interestingly enough, modern-day Chicago has one known exorcist, whereas Italy is reputed to have nearly 400.

In my estimation, Father Canning did not perform an exorcism on that day he retrieved the consecrated hosts from the attic of the Saint Charles rectory. The act of exorcism is more complex, more mysterious and is directed at evil. Some exorcisms take weeks, even months. Perhaps the noises from the third floor came from a good spirit calling on someone to rectify the improper preservation of the Eucharist. Starting back then, that spirit was presumed to be Muldoon.

Chapter Sixteen

Kane's Last Chance

AFTER MONSIGNOR CANNING bartered his way out of Saint Charles, Father John McMahon became the next pastor in 1941. After him, Pastor Kane was assigned in 1952. During this period in time, the legend of Muldoon quietly grew among the clergy who lived at the rectory and experienced other unexplainable manifestations. And then there was me—the lone and green assistant of a burned-out pastor living in a haunted rectory. Just weeks into my first assignment I was left without the friendship of a fellow assistant, alone to deal with Pastor Kane, his domineering housekeeper, Irma, and his spoiled dog, Duke. For the most part, I had the entire lonely second floor all to myself. The rooms for other assistants sat eerily dark and deserted, while the immense bathroom for three priests and the lone phone in the hallway was at my sole disposal. Meanwhile, every night, Kane and Duke would lock themselves into the suite at the front of the rectory.

One Sunday night I was alone having supper in the rectory with the pastor. Being at home for supper with Kane was not easy. He was often morose and so angry. Kane usually moved through the meal in minutes with little to say, unless it was about bingo or his collection of cut glass, though he might obsess about his fears of Muldoon. But tonight it was a different story. He sat at the table with a stubborn resolve on his face, and I couldn't quite figure out what was going on. Had I done something to upset him? Was I in trouble again? With Duke sitting at his right-hand side, he asked me a question: "Rocco, has anyone called you about the medical center?"

"No. What about it?" I asked.

"Good. I spoke with Cardinal Stritch and told him that we weren't interested in hospital ministry. We have too much to do here." I could tell that Kane had made up his mind. The pastor, who had already shunned the black and poor parishioners in the community, now was refusing to get involved with the hospital ministry growing around us.

The West Side Medical Center really started to develop in 1884, a year before Saint Charles was founded, when the Cook County Hospital and Rush Medical College opened their doors at Harrison and Wood Streets. Before World War I, the right of eminent domain was claiming more and more residential blocks for hospitals and auxiliary medical institutions. Even America's favorite pastime couldn't get in the way of the growth. The West Side Grounds, the baseball field where the Chicago White Stockings played their games from 1893 to 1915, across from the Holy Trinity rectory on Lincoln (now Wolcott) between Taylor and Polk Streets, was taken over by the Illinois Research Hospital's building complex. (The ball club, officially renamed the Chicago Cubs in 1907, moved in 1916 to a new ball park, which would later be named Wrigley Field, at Clark and Addison Streets.) Since

The original Holy Trinity Parish at Taylor Street and Wolcott Avenue. (Reprinted from *Souvenir of the Archdiocese of Chicago, Commemorating the Installation of the Most Reverend George W. Mundelein, D.D. February 19, 1916.*)

those early days, the landscape of the burgeoning medical center changed almost every day. By 1956 the countless homes east of Damen all the way to Ashland had been leveled for the construction of new hospitals and related institutions.

Like Saint Charles, Holy Trinity was founded in 1885 and stood at Taylor and Lincoln. At the time, it was a German parish organized within the limits of the territorial parish of Saint Charles Borromeo. Eventually, Holy Trinity was faced with the same challenges for growth and survival on Chicago's West Side. Gentrification, decreased Catholic enrollment, and the influx of poor immigrants were leading to the decline of both parishes. By 1951 Holy Trinity served only one block, Winchester Avenue, comprising mostly Italians who occupied the few buildings standing there. In the middle of the 1950s, plans for demolition were set, directing the newly developing hospital ministry to the most logical choice, Saint Charles Borromeo, which stood in the very heart of the new hospital district. But unlike Saint Charles, Holy Trinity was searching for a Catholic population to serve and was willing to adapt for survival.

As Pastor Kane continued, neither of us realized how significant his next statements would be. "We're not getting overloaded with that mess. Let Holy Trinity deal with it. If anyone calls, tell them we're not getting involved."

As if to punctuate Kane's statement, the outside door of the hallway connecting the rectory and the church suddenly slammed shut. Duke immediately ran to the door and started barking at the closed doorway, and Irma came out of the kitchen to see what was going on. Then we heard heavy footsteps pounding from the side entrance, like someone was running through the passageway into the church. This was alarming and puzzling, as I had double-locked the outside door of the passageway after baptismal time earlier that afternoon. Pastor Kane opened the side door and hurried into the church with Irma and Duke. Everything was dark. Even the sanctuary lamp, the candle that was perpetually lit to signify the presence of Christ, had been snuffed out. Duke had quit barking and was strolling through the church, just wagging his tail. I began to turn on every light in the immense space to help us find a perpetrator, and as Pastor Kane quickly reprimanded me for wasting electricity, he and Irma locked the doors. With the interior illuminated by the only four lights that I had permission to turn on, we systematically searched the entire building: the main nave, the vestibules, the pews, sacristies, confessionals, and every other place someone could hide. No one was there.

We relit the sanctuary lamp, and after about an hour or so, we double-checked the locked doors once again, turned off the electric lights, and returned to the rectory. As we secured the church and rectory, Pastor Kane didn't say a word. When we were finished, he went straight to the breakfast nook, fed Duke the remains of our cold meal, then went to his room with the dog and locked the door behind them. From Kane's silence, I could tell that he was also disturbed by not being able to explain what we heard that evening. We all went to bed that night wondering if this was Muldoon once again.

After Kane insisted to Cardinal Stritch that there was already too much to do at Saint Charles, a new pastor was installed at Holy Trinity and demolition plans were temporarily halted. Father John Marren was sent over from Holy Name Cathedral, and with the help of two assistants, Fathers Ed Norkett and Bill Riordan, they would serve the sick and the dying in the surrounding hospitals. The old, small, and obsolete Holy Trinity Church was leveled, and a new parish center was constructed for the needs of an escalating hospital community.

I've reflected upon the odd events of that day time and again. By turning down the opportunity of ministering to the West Side Medical Center, Pastor Kane literally sounded the death knell of Saint Charles Borromeo, and I believe that Muldoon was there to protest the impending doom of his magnificent church.

∞

In general, Duke was a dog with a mild temperament, treated better by Kane than were any of the assistants at Saint Charles. Duke was well fed and pampered by Irma, truly living a "dog's life." He was very loyal to the pastor, coming to his aid whenever he sensed that Kane was being threatened. Like most any dog, he would bark and growl and even attack when he sensed something just wasn't right. I remember one occasion when a stranger approached Kane and Duke as they entered the rear of the rectory. Duke immediately came to his owner's defense, exposing his fangs and literally chasing the vagrant down the block until he felt that Pastor Kane was out of harm's way.

Could Duke see what was beyond the reach of humans? Could he see the rectory ghost? I believe that Duke was sensitive to the manifestations of Muldoon. This stands to reason, as animals, with their naturally sharper senses of hearing and smell than those of humans, can sense intruders. During my third year at Saint Charles, the two assistants, the resident, and Pastor Kane were finishing supper one night when there was a lull in the conversation. During that silence, the heavy front door of the rectory slammed shut. We looked at each other, waiting for the situation to develop, figuring that someone who had a key was coming in. Who could this be? Then the second door leading to the rest of the rectory, just a few feet from the dining room, also opened and shut hard. We all heard it. With that Duke quickly rose to his feet, pranced into the entryway, and looked into the hall to see who had entered. Duke just stood there, pleasantly wagging his tail. Seconds later, we heard heavy footsteps of someone climbing the squeaky stairs to the second floor. We rose as one from the table and looked to the stairway to find no one there. After a quick investigation and coming up with nothing, we returned to our places realizing that Duke had seen something that we could not. Though none of us can see the world through a dog's eyes, it was my thought that Duke's calm reaction was a result of being able to see Muldoon.

Chapter Seventeen

The Back Room

ON WEDNESDAY, JULY 25, 1956, startling news broke on TVs and radios nationwide. In a dense fog and the night's darkness off the northeast U.S. coast near Nantucket Island, the exquisite Italian passenger ship the *Andrea Doria* collided with a Swedish liner. The *Stockholm*, which had been built with a reinforced hull to withstand the ice floes of the north, hit the *Andrea Doria* broadside while it was traveling from Naples to New York City. The collision left a massive hole in the *Andrea Doria*'s bow, causing it to sink to the bottom of the Atlantic early the next day. In the dark of night, 1,705 passengers and crew on board the *Andrea Doria* scrambled to save themselves from the devouring sea. Between both ships, only 51 lives were lost, and 2,401 people were saved. It was said to be the greatest sea rescue in history.

Four of the survivors of the *Andrea Doria* shipwreck were Chicago priests. One was a classmate of mine, Tom

Kelly, who experienced his major seminary theological training and ordination to the priesthood in Rome. The other three were postgraduate students who earned additional degrees in Rome for specialized work in the Archdiocese of Chicago. There was Father John Dolciamore, who served at Saint Charles at one time, and Father Richard Wojcik. Completing the fortunate quartet was Father Raymond E. Goedert, who had been an assistant priest at Saint Gabriel's on the city's South Side. Ray received a degree in canon law and was destined to work in the Chancery Office. Everything that Father Goedert and the others owned was loaded on the *Andrea Doria* before it embarked from Naples and found itself at the murky bottom of the cold, dark Atlantic. Once on land, all that they had was the clothes on their backs and the gift of their lives spared from the sea. Father Goedert was sent to Saint Attracta's in Cicero as a resident priest while working at the Chancery Office during the day. Those arrangements changed quickly.

It was a Wednesday afternoon in August later that same year. My day off. I was visiting a friend of mine, Emil Serafini, a young seminarian from Our Lady of the Angels. Like my father, Emil's dad had come from the same small Italian city of Sora di Frosinone and had little liking for the Church. Having similar backgrounds, Emil and I had a lot to talk about. We were traveling west on the Division Street auto bus; I was sitting at an open window on the driver's side of the vehicle. All of a sudden, I felt a smack to my left eye. By the time I put my hand up, blood was already streaming down my face and I could only see out of my right eye. A few neighborhood boys were standing on the curb throwing rocks and mud balls mixed with stones at the passing bus—I had been pelted. The bus suddenly stopped, and the boys fled in all directions. The driver came back to see my injury, then turned off of his route and drove a few sympathetic passengers, Emil, and me to the nearest hospital, where I was diagnosed with permanent damage to the left eye—blurred vision, like looking through wax paper. The story made the gossip column in the *Chicago Daily News*. As a result, I had to spend a week in darkness and did so at my sister Theresa's house, getting me out of the rectory for a bit.

Pastor Kane was not pleased to learn about my accident. With me incapacitated and no other priests in the rectory, Kane was left to attend to all the administrative and religious matters of Saint Charles by himself. He was irate. The pastor appealed to the chancery for help, and they responded by moving Father Goedert from Saint Attracta's to Saint Charles. Ray's assignment was to continue his daily work at the Chancery Office, while residing at Saint Charles so he could at least provide some auxiliary support to Pastor Kane until I got better.

Upon my return to the rectory, Kane milked my injury for all it was worth, especially to the Tuesday night bingo crowd. Though I was a bit depressed about partially losing my eyesight and was sheepish about having to wear a bandage over my eye while it was healing, Father Kane saw an angle to help generate revenue for the parish. Against my wishes, the pastor insisted that I come down to the bingo hall dressed in my cassock, wearing dark glasses over the patch on my left eye, and carrying a cane—which I didn't need—in my right hand. Kane had me stand in the center of the bingo stage, where, with a microphone in one hand and pointing at me with the other, he exploited sympathy from the crowd by telling them to look at "poor Father Rocco." I had been degraded to a cheap sideshow attraction.

Father Goedert had moved into the second-floor back room at the end of the rectory. He was gone every working weekday and most weekday evenings working on other assignments, like the NAIM organization for widows and widowers. (Naim is a Biblical town where Jesus raises a widow's son from the dead.) Father Goedert was a busy man and wasn't around that much. He was also a good man who worked well with other people. Coming from a large family of 12, his edges had been smoothed over and he was easy to live with. When I had my run-ins with Kane, I could confide in Ray; he heard me out. Though I never told him, Raymond Goedert was my mainstay and model during my difficult years at Saint Charles Borromeo. It was good to have him in the house.

The only door to Father Goedert's room was directly across from my study door. His quarters consisted of a single room facing away from Hoyne Avenue. It had two average size windows, one of which faced the parochial school to the north; the other faced the brick sacristy of the church, which looked out over a small courtyard. The back room had a double bed with a sofa chair next to it; an unadorned wooden desk sat in the corner. There were a couple of lamps on separate circuits, an overhead light with a wall switch, and a small radio. It was nothing fancy.

It was about 9 P.M. on Sunday night, and I was home alone. The pastor, Irma, and Duke were just returning from an automobile ride outside the neighborhood to enjoy the fresh night air. Kane and Irma were inseparable. Their routine was the same every Sunday—finish a short supper, escape together from the parish boundaries for a few hours, then return in a fashion they believed was inconspicuous. Sometimes he would come into the rectory first, then Irma would come in with Duke about ten minutes later. Everyone could tell they were spending time together. On this particular night, I heard Kane's loud and creaky footsteps all the way from my study. I was doing some light reading when I thought I'd walk down the hall to inform him of Monday morning's Mass schedule. I had notified Saint Pius V on Ashland Avenue to send us an additional priest because we had a rare and unexpected funeral the next day, and we needed some help.

As I walked out of my study, I noticed that the door to Father Goedert's room was wide open; the space was as black as my cassock and filled with a deafening silence that spilled out into the corridor. I walked the other way down the hall and knocked at Kane's closed door. Through the door, I let the pastor know that the slots for Monday morning Mass were filled. Kane harrumphed "Okay" back to me through the closed entryway. By the time I turned around and walked back down the hall, I could see bright light pouring out from Father Goedert's room. His doorway was now glowing with intense brilliance, and as I walked slowly to the back of the rectory, I heard the growing sound of classical music. When I looked into Ray's room, I found that every light in the room was turned on. There were two table lamps plugged into independent outlets, an overhead light was turned on by a wall switch, and Ray's table radio was filling the room with classical music from WGN. What the heck was going on? I shouted from the hall, "Ray? Are you home?" No reply. I walked into the open bathroom next to Ray's single room—he wasn't there.

Without touching anything, I hurried back down the hall to inform the pastor of what was happening. After I told Kane that the back room was filled with light and music with no one there to turn on the switches, he looked at me nervously and said, "It's Muldoon . . . he's done this one before. He must be up to something." With that, Kane closed his door in my face and locked it behind him.

I walked back down the corridor to the room at the back of the rectory and turned off the radio and the lights, returning Ray's room to its darkened state. Father Goedert returned home at about 10 P.M. and poked his head into my study. "Hey, Rock, what's going on?" I sure had a story to share with him!

Less than two weeks later, I was asked to bring Holy Communion to a young housewife who was in the late stages of pregnancy and confined to bed rest. Anna had been married in our church and used to work as the afternoon secretary at Saint Charles under the pastorate of Monsignor John McMahon. She lived a few blocks away in a three-flat on Oakley Boulevard just south of Taylor Street. When I arrived, a caretaker let me in. Anna's first-floor apartment was well prepared for her reception of Communion. There was a small table covered with white linen upon which stood a crucifix flanked by two lighted candles next to her sick bed. We exchanged pleasantries and spoke for a short while. After I had administered the Sacrament, the weak and tired Anna asked me to talk with her for a bit longer.

"Father, can I ask you something?'

"Sure. What is it?"

"When I worked in the rectory a few years ago, there was a room at the back of the rectory. . . ." She struggled for a deep breath and to gather her thoughts. "The priests said that the lights would turn on and off, and the radio would come on. I overheard them say a couple of times that it was the ghost of a priest or something. I never believed it . . . until one night, when no one was around, I heard the radio all of a sudden. The music was coming from upstairs. I heard it all the way from the office." She stopped and yawned.

Though I was pretty spooked by her story, I remained calm and urged her to continue. "What did you do? Were you scared?"

"Yeah, I was scared. I couldn't figure out who else was in the rectory. When Father McMahon came home, I told him what happened. From what I remember, he had an electrician come take a look at it . . . but everything checked out okay. Do you think it was a ghost?"

We talked a bit more, and I eventually skirted Anna's question by blessing her and her unborn child. She soon fell softly asleep. Her body needed rest for the baby she carried within her. I quietly let myself out, never telling Anna what I had witnessed in the back room only weeks before.

∞

During the process of writing this book, my wife and I had Bishop Goedert over for dinner to talk about the good old days. In our discussion, Bishop Goedert would not openly admit that the ghost of Muldoon haunted the rectory of Saint Charles. And given the official stance of the Catholic Church on the existence of ghosts, I don't think he could. What he did admit was that a lot of "strange things" he could not explain did take place there, like sounds of dressers rolling on the packed attic floor above us, crashing night noises coming from the kitchen, and other "weird and strange happenings." He also told me that he once received a call from a priest in the Diocese of Rockford. He wanted to know about the strange happenings that took place in the Saint Charles rectory after the death of Muldoon in 1927. Apparently, through word of mouth, the legend of Muldoon has spread.

Chapter Eighteen

A Light Under A Basket

TO THE RECOLLECTION OF HIS peers, William A. Schumacher was considered the most illuminated mind ever to move through the seminary system of the Archdiocese of Chicago. Bill outshone the other intellectual lights of the graduating class of 1954, such as Tom Bowler, Andrew Greeley, Marty Hegarty, Gene McClory, Howard Tuite—all acknowledged by the student body as illuminati, the brightest lights. The genius of Father Schumacher was his ability to understand the most complex concepts coupled with his superlative gift of total recall. An avid reader, Bill understood and remembered everything that he had ever studied, down to the very last detail. Father Schumacher was a scholar in the purest sense of the word.

Bill's intelligence and photographic memory towered over the entire seminary population. It also pulled many struggling third-year philosophy students through the toughest class of the most demanding teacher on the seminary's philosophy faculty, the Reverend Raymond Dunst, S.J., whose quick and active movements earned him the nickname Shakey. Shakey Dunst was so well versed in teaching philosophy, he rarely taught from the assigned text of the French Jesuit philosopher Charles Boyer. His classes were conducted almost exclusively in Latin and were based upon his own free-form lecture. Out of the blue, he would discuss the theories of main Catholic philosophers like Saint Thomas Aquinas, then bounce to the teachings of adversaries such as Kant, Descartes, Hegel, and so many others. When Shakey spoke, he expected us to understand his every word; as he would if he were talking casually to other doctors of philosophy, he provided little background or explanation. But it often was way over our heads. He gave only a half dozen tests a semester, and the exams were so tough that virtually no one came close to even a passing grade. Of the few people to ever fully understand Shakey Dunst's class was Bill Schumacher. When in Shakey's class, Bill used his photographic memory to transcribe Dunst's rapid-fire notes to paper after every lecture. During the study period following the class, Bill would bang away on his old typewriter, transcribing the previous philosophy lecture. He mimeographed these extensive and detailed notes and shared them not only with his classmates but also with the continuous classes of seminarians that followed him. If you were to sit in Shakey's class, you would be able to follow his lecture concept for concept, almost word for word, from Bill's notes. Two years behind Bill in the seminary, I used a copy of his notes to get me through, and I still have them in a thick black binder in my small library.

In spite of his intellectual brilliance, Bill Schumacher lacked basic social skills. He was impatient. Many times he was condescending. Known as a pure choleric with an explosive temper, he had only a few personal friends. Those who knew him well were aware of his sensitivity that hid behind a severe and impregnable German facade. During meals as a post-graduate, he sat with the faculty, and the student waiters went out of their way to avoid him. He could be known to complain when service was not fast or efficient enough. I remember him once growling to the young philosophers, "Move faster, or I'll have you castrated with a rusty old tin can!" His caustic remarks often rippled through the entertainment-starved student body. As funny as his comments were though, no one wanted to be on the receiving end of his wrath. Everyone stayed clear of Schumacher.

After ordination, Father Schumacher was not sent to a parish as was the rest of his class, but instead he was selected to remain in the seminary as a postgraduate student, which indicated that one day he would teach in the seminary system or he would apply his many intellectual skills to work in the chancery. Father Schumacher breezed through his two-year postgraduate study, writing a brilliant dissertation—"Spiritus and Spiritualis: A Study in the Sermons of Saint Augustine"—which was published in 1957. Armed with his doctrinal ring, which he always wore on his left hand, the Reverend William A. Schumacher was ready for his first assignment. The question was, *Where would he be sent?* This brilliant man, who was endowed with tremendous abstract and theoretical skills, had the people skills of a block of lead. Who could tolerate working with him? The Church decided to send Bill to a place where he could do the least harm. Not to the seminary or the chancery or any of its archdiocesan offices, but to the lowliest place in the diocese.

Because Father Goedert's primary duty was to the chancery, there was still a need to fill the open spot left by Father Gaughn. Father Schumacher was appointed as assistant to Saint Charles Borromeo during the fall of 1956. Bill and I worked on a few projects together in the seminary, and I was happy he was coming. By now I was about four months into my first assignment, and I had experienced quite a bit on my own. But despite my personal desire for there to be another assistant at Saint Charles, I couldn't help wondering why the chancery was burying Father Schumacher among people with no intellectual skills, why this brilliant light was being covered with a basket. Saint Charles was filled with hardworking people, the unskilled, and the poorest of every ethnic group. I knew of only a few in the parish who had completed college, yet so many who could not read or write. It was a challenge for a neighborhood student even to finish eight years of grammar school, or at the most to complete high school. There were no study groups in the parish or book discussion clubs in the community. There was absolutely nothing to challenge a mental whiz—just pervasive illiteracy. At first I thought the diocese had made another of its personnel mistakes. Bill, however, following his promise of obedience and accepting what he termed "God's will," calmly and humbly immersed himself into working for the poor.

Father Schumacher moved in and took Father Gaughn's former quarters, transforming the study into a massive library with books in shelves that rose from the floor to the ten-foot high ceiling. At times, Bill would read a book a day about what was going on in the world, the big issues of human rights, politics, and the ethics of inequality, which he witnessed in our locale every day. Almost surprisingly, Bill and I got along great. Where I was amazed at how smart and well read he was, Bill was a bit fascinated by me as well. He took a shine to me because I was the improbable street kid who had come into the priesthood from a tough Italian neighborhood, and he laughed heartily at my tales of the small-time mobsters I knew from my old neighborhood, like Marty the Ox, Needle-nose, Thirty-pieces, and Sammy J. I think he felt that I had what he didn't have—basic street smarts and people skills.

Over the next few years, Bill Schumacher and I talked at length of the suffering that took place within our parish. We also frequently spoke about the strange things that happened within the church and rectory of Saint Charles Borromeo that we attributed to the ghost of Muldoon. One of these strange things had to do with the wall in my room. It wasn't a load-bearing wall that hid pipes, electrical wiring, or telephone lines, just a wall used to divide space, separating my room from the rectory corridor. One morning I inadvertently touched the wall and immediately had cause to pull back. The wall was red-hot. I carefully touched it with the palms of both hands. The wall was burning, as if there was a fire inside it. I went downstairs and interrupted Bill's breakfast, asking him to touch the wall, but this time it was as cold as the inside of an icebox—a complete switch of temperatures in a very short span of time. We both experienced this again on different occasions, as it happened from time to time during my four years at Saint Charles.

Over the time we spent together, I could see a transformation in Bill, from being a theorist to becoming a champion of the underdogs who lived in our impoverished parochial society. Father Schumacher studied the poor and became fascinated by their plight, resolving to assist them whenever he could. He worked vigorously to help the destitute and the homeless, taking charge of the Holy Name Society and the ever busy Saint Vincent DePaul Society that took care of the poor in extreme difficulty. During the week, Bill collected second- and third-hand clothes and canned goods to be distributed from the basement of the school during the weekends. A great change took place in his personality. Bill became more human.

An example of Bill's new humanity that remains etched in my memory happened one cold winter's night in late November, about 7:30 P.M. There was scarcely any traffic on Roosevelt Road. Most people were huddled inside their homes, perhaps warming themselves around a small fire from a potbelly stove or near a gas oven, its doors open for the heat. Bill was on duty that night when the front doorbell of the rectory rang. Dressed in a black cassock, Father Schumacher opened the door to be blasted with the icy winter weather and the foulest smell from the man standing in the entrance. It was Old Man Casey, a Madison Street derelict, who regularly rang our doorbell looking for a break from the elements, for perhaps a sandwich or a pair of gloves, or maybe 50 cents for some cheap wine and a bed for the night in a flophouse on Madison Street. Each of the priests in the rectory had come to know Casey well and all knew he smelled bad. He never bathed. His clothes were tattered and thin. His blotched baldhead was beet red. His teeth chattered. His nose ran continuously. When Bill opened the door, the thick smell of body odor and filth virtually flattened him.

Bill invited Casey in from the inclement conditions and ushered him into the small front office of the rectory. Standing before Father Schumacher, the forsaken Casey, shaking from frigid discomfort, began to cry. To worsen this pitiful scene, Casey's bladder released, soaking his trousers with the stream of urine that puddled around his worn shoes and onto the old curled linoleum floor. In another day, Schumacher would have lost his temper, scolded Casey with truck-driver vulgarities for defiling the rectory, and thrown the old man out on his ear. Now though, Father Schumacher provided comfort, getting Casey a new set of clean clothes from the Saint Vincent DePaul storage, then sat him down in the rectory's kitchen for a hot cup of coffee and a sandwich. After this, Father Schumacher reached into his pocket, gave the consoled Casey some change to find a warm place to sleep for the night, and watched the beaten old man disappear into the cold night air. Then Bill filled a bucket with hot soapy water, got down on his knees, and thoroughly scrubbed the puddle Casey had left on the rectory floor. Later that evening, Bill and I were alone when he told me of Old Man Casey's visit. I looked at him quietly as he narrated what had happened. I was awestruck and deeply moved at his outstanding act of charity for a Madison Street bum. Here was a doctor of theology involved in a task that would be menial to a hospital attendant, yet Bill's compassion had turned the incident to gold.

The most graphic of the Muldoon stories regarding Father Schumacher took place after Bill had returned from a two-week vacation in Mexico, when he was struck with a nasty bout of Montezuma's Revenge. As a result, he spent many days isolated in his room recovering from nausea and dysentery. Toward the end of his illness, Father Schumacher came down to breakfast after being holed up in his room for days. The first morning I saw him, Bill barked at me, "What the hell were you doing outside my bedroom door last night?"

I looked at him quizzically. "What are you talking about?"

Bill went on, "Damn it, I was dead asleep, Rock. I've been feeling awful and I need to get my rest! What was that, a bowling ball?"

"I have no idea what you are talking about!" I emphatically replied.

"Last night it sounded like you were bouncing a bowling ball up and down on the floor outside my bedroom door. The pounding was driving me nuts. And where did you get those chains you were banging against my door frame?"

"Are you serious?" I said. "Bill, I slept the entire night . . . and where would I get a bowling ball and a set of chains? What time did this happen?"

"About 1:30 in the morning."

"Well, I know it wasn't me," I insisted. Befuddled, we both sat there and pondered what had happened.

"Then who the hell was it?" He looked at me with eyes widened from revelation. "Do you think it was Muldoon?"

With no other explanation of what happened, we both concluded that it was.

∞

Before going any further, it's important to mention that both Father Goedert and Father Schumacher were very cynical of the possibility that a ghost was haunting Saint Charles. Although they both admitted that a lot of bizarre, unexplainable things went on at the rectory, neither was ready yet to acknowledge that these happenings originated from Muldoon's presence. After all, both of them were smart and educated individuals. Because of their philosophical training, they were skeptical, trained to suspend judgment until all the evidence was in. They wanted cold, hard facts. They were also well versed in Catholic doctrine that does not officially support the existence of ghosts. The thought that a ghost caused all of these strange things to happen just didn't make sense. Understandably, they weren't going to just take my word for it. So, whenever the front oak doors suddenly slammed shut or the hardwood floors squeaked from footsteps, Father Schumacher and I, who were home more than Father Goedert, researched the cause of the noise. We questioned everything in search of a natural reason for the many unusual happenings. Perhaps some of the rectory's noises were coming from the settling of the massive stone structure in the muddy ground beneath its foundation. Kane had let the place deteriorate so much it was possible that the metal anchors in the old plaster walls were just bound to give way. A short circuit could have been the cause of the sudden burst of electricity in the back room. Maybe we had taken the Muldoon legend too seriously. Or perhaps Goedert and Schumacher would need more contact with the paranormal to be convinced . . . like I already had.

I remember one Monday morning, as I prepared to go over to the grammar school to speak to the children who had missed Sunday Mass the day before, there was a knock on my bedroom door. It was Father Schumacher, who came immediately to my room after celebrating the last Mass of the morning. He had something on his mind.

"Rock, follow me. Let's not talk right now. Just tell me if you detect anything unusual." Bill led me through the rectory and into the church, behind the main altar where Muldoon at one time had planned to be buried. Father Schumacher looked me and asked, "Do you notice anything?"

"Well," I replied, "I'm wondering where this smell of flowers is coming from." The smell of lilacs was pungent, like I was standing in the middle of a flower garden. But there were no flowers in sight. In fact, flowers were purchased only on rare occasions in our parish, almost exclusively for Christmas and Easter.

Bill was floored. He, too, smelled the flowers and couldn't explain where the scent was coming from. Without his prompting me, I confirmed exactly what he had detected on his own. Bill didn't really say much after my response, but from that day forward I think he really began believing in the legend of Muldoon.

Chapter Nineteen

The Withered Tree

And seeing a fig tree by the wayside, he came up to it and found nothing on it but leaves: and he said to it, "May no fruit ever come to thee, hence forward forever." And immediately, the fig tree withered up.

—Matthew 22:19–20

BILL SCHUMACHER RELISHED being the protector of the Tuesday night bingo collections. Like Father Gaughn before him, Schumacher's bingo duty was picking up the admission receipts from the bingo cage in the church hall. But Bill's style was a little bit different. While Father Gaughn carried the bag of money himself, Father Schumacher preferred that a parish volunteer carry the cash, while Bill followed in an unbuttoned suit coat, always ready to draw his revolver. He called his handgun "the equalizer" seeing that it put him on the same level as the predators in the community. Bill didn't carry his revolver all the time, but when he did, it was in a small holster on the inside of his belt, so he would be quick on the draw if he needed it. I remember that being armed even came in handy on one occasion. Bill and the volunteer bagman exited the church basement into the small courtyard leading to the rectory's rear entrance when two armed men came from out of the shadows, demanding that they turn over the evening's income. Father Schumacher slowly drew his gun, and when the steel blue metal barrel shone underneath the single courtyard light, the two robbers realized they were being challenged and fled. At first, I was very disillusioned that a priest, a man of peace, would possess and carry a gun. But after working in this struggling community for some time, I could understand his rationale.

At the corner of Michigan Avenue and Roosevelt Road there once stood the Illinois Central Railroad Terminal, which played a large role in the great migration of people in the late 1800s. The Illinois Central Railroad ran north from New Orleans, flooding the city with poor migrants, predominantly black. They came just as other immigrants did, carrying only a few belongings, the clothes on their backs, and enough food to last a day or two. When they climbed aboard the train in Louisiana, the many African-American passengers had to sit in the Jim Crow seats, which were segregated by color until the train reached Cincinnati, whereupon passengers were free to sit anywhere they chose. Those long trains discharged unnumbered southerners into the massive city, exposing them to unaccustomed traffic and a different, urban way of life that was unlike anything they had ever experienced before. The Valley easily became home to the many transient travelers looking to establish themselves in the up-and-coming metropolis. Thousands trickled into the area south of Roosevelt Road, where rent was low in the dense grouping of nineteenth-century buildings—most of them deteriorated, few maintained with care, paint, or cleaning. Work was available in the many factories at the Valley's south end. Even at very low wages, unskilled laborers new to the area eagerly responded to the need of the hiring factories and the railroad. The combination of poverty, ignorance, and a transient population made the Valley an unfortunate and dangerous place to live.

One morning, a young black Southern woman in her early 30s visited me at the rectory, requesting that I come to her apartment as soon as possible to baptize her infant daughter, who had died shortly after birth. Leaving the rectory as soon as possible, I walked to her apartment near 13th Street and Damen Avenue. From the suspended wooden sidewalk, I descended a wooden stairway below street level, through a gangway between buildings, to a destitute backyard. There were no flowers, no bushes, no grass. The impacted ground was littered with garbage like broken bottles, paper wrappers, and leftover animal bones. Running around in the yard were two old emaciated street dogs sniffing for food.

I ascended the rear stairs of the woman's apartment; she met me at the door with three mourners at her side. I was led to the mother's only bedroom, where the body of the tiny baby girl, covered to her neck by battleship gray bedsheets, looked like a bump on the large double bed. I baptized her conditionally for the comfort of her mother and her friends. The Sacrament, the words of Scripture, and the prayers of the Church seemed to comfort the small group of mourners. Because the mother was virtually destitute, I directed her to come to the church where the aid of the Catholic Charities could be of assistance, at least to purchase a small white coffin and a burial place for the infant. With a shocking reply to my offer, she responded, "You don't have to do all that, Father. I'll bury her next to her brother, in the backyard, like I did two years ago."

Another story concerns two young Southern brothers who came to Chicago lacking basic urban knowledge. Before going to bed one night in their small apartment in the Valley, they blew out the flames of two gas wall sconces. They didn't even think to turn out the flames using the gas shut-off valve. They died the first night they were in town.

On Easter Sunday of 1957, a police car stopped at the rectory to report a gruesome crime that had taken place just a few blocks away from Saint Charles Borromeo. Marshall Abraham worked as a butcher in the stockyards and had no previous record of violence. Then one night, Abraham attacked Anna Jones, his live-in girlfriend and the mother of their three children. After chasing Anna about three blocks, Abraham tackled her in the street, stabbing her about ten times in the back with his hunting knife. Then, using the curb as a chopping block, he precisely severed her head from her body. Abraham carried the head a few blocks to 1638 W. Roosevelt Road, where he threw it into a wire trash basket. While there have been numerous cases of dismemberments in police history, this was the first known where the gory butchering took place in public. The *Chicago Defender* deemed Abraham "the Mad Butcher."

Father Goedert, Father Schumacher, and I talked at length of these and the many other unfortunate happenings that took place in our troubled and seemingly insensitive community. Strangely, these sad occurrences had no effect on the people living in the Valley, almost as if the poverty, the robberies, and the murders were all expected in this part of town, and the residents were left to tolerate it stoically.

The fact that most blacks from the South were predominantly Baptists, Methodists, or Evangelicals was devastating to the Catholic parish of Saint Charles. Blacks and a sprinkling of Hispanics and Eastern Europeans now replaced the thousands of Irish Catholics who had lived within the parish boundaries for decades. Saint Charles lost its core of parishioners, which was evident through the entire ministry. During the reign of Bishop Muldoon, the parochial grammar school peaked at a student body of 1,200 children, which now had diminished to about 500 students, half of whom were not Catholic. And enrollment continued to dwindle. The parish life during the Muldoon days, which boasted many Masses overflowing with parishioners every Sunday and more than 20 parish societies catering to every segment of the Catholic community, had withered away. Despite the depleted Catholic population, Pastor Kane maintained the old schedules for the parish. With congregants or without, the scheduling of the parish would remain the same. There were still five Masses every Sunday regardless of attendance. On Saturdays, we would still sit in the confessional box for long afternoon and evening hours with only a handful of penitents between two priests. I often brought a book with me to pass the time.

Pastor Kane was terrified of Saint Charles's West Side community. He didn't leave the safety of the rectory too often. Fearful of the slum neighborhood, Kane had developed a siege mentality and was drawing us into his apprehensions of reaching out to the greater population. One of Pastor Kane's biggest fears was a break-in at the church. He thought that someone unfamiliar with Catholic Church furnishings might think the golden door of the tabernacle was a safe for holding valuable treasures of the parish. To warn us of any thieves, Kane installed an alarm bell behind the grandfather clock at the stairs ascending to the rectory's second floor. The alarm was connected to a large pad underneath an Oriental rug on the platform before the main altar of the church. If someone was to approach the tabernacle while the alarm was on, everyone in the house would know. It was the function of the priest who celebrated the first Mass in the morning to trip the switch so as not to wake up the entire house with the resounding alarm bell.

One afternoon while I was on duty, I was in my room at my desk, waiting for an appointment to arrive, while Father Schumacher was sitting in his study reading one of his countless books. The alarm bell, which was the size of a dinner plate, rang furiously. Someone was on the platform of the main altar. Immediately, I jumped to my feet and dashed through the rectory to the side entrance of the church, where I saw a tall man trying to break into the tabernacle. Bill Schumacher followed me by about 20 feet; he wasn't carrying his gun. I shouted at the intruder, "What are you doing here?" With that the prowler let out a bloodcurdling howl, ran from the main altar, hurdled the communion rail, and dashed down the center aisle like he was an Olympic athlete. He then hurled himself through the closed interior doors of the vestibule and descended the marble stairs to the outside doors of the church. I was just steps behind him, racing down the side aisle. I caught up with the intruder as he reached the outside center doors, which were locked. As I raced down the stairs, trapping the intruder against the locked doors, I steadied myself by grabbing the brass handrail in the middle of the front stairway with my left hand. Trying to escape, the intruder bounced off the locked door, then turned at me and made an overhand lunge with his knife, just grazing my right shoulder but slicing my cassock. He had come perilously close to cutting me with that swing. I stood there in shock. Having halted my pursuit, the intruder ran to the east side entrance, where he must have entered the church in the first place, and escaped. Bill was shouting from the main altar, "Rock, let him go. The tabernacle's okay. He didn't get anything." After being assaulted, in a church of all places, I watched my attacker dash in and out of traffic on Roosevelt Road as he disappeared into the Valley.

∞

During his time at Saint Charles Borromeo, Father Schumacher wrote an article for the Jesuit magazine America, titled "On Loving the Poor," which is printed in its entirety in Appendix D of this book. Bill made a strong point in that article about how it is all too easy to just write a check to support the poor but that it is more important to deal with the poor directly. The latter provides the giver with an understanding of the plight of those who live in need. Father Schumacher enacted this principle during the Christmas season of 1958. A classmate of mine, Father John Hurley of Our Lady of Loretto parish in Hometown, Illinois, had organized a food collection, part of which was destined for the poor of Saint Charles. When I told Bill of the generous offer baskets of food from the people of the far-off suburban parish, he was delighted. But he added the stipulation that with the acceptance of the scores of food baskets, some of the men of Hometown would have to help make the deliveries to poor families in our community.

On a Sunday night two weeks before Christmas at about 8 P.M., a crew from Hometown came to distribute their gifts. Each man from Our Lady of Loretto was teamed with a parishioner from Saint Charles to deliver large parcels of food and other Christmas treats throughout the neighborhood. One delivery took place on the third-floor flat of a dark block on 14th Street and Winchester, tucked in the depths of the Valley. The night was bitter cold and dark. The dim streetlights seemed inadequate. There were no Christmas lights or signs of festivity anywhere on this barren moonscape. After finding the address, the twosome used a flashlight to find their way to the rear stairway of the three-story building. This was turning out to be a scary experience. The two men began their slow ascent of the rear stairs with the basket between them, each with a hand on its wire handle lifting the basket slowly, from one wooden stair to another, in almost pitch-black darkness. Once they were only one floor from the final destination, the man from Hometown lifted the basket to his right shoulder to go the final flight alone. When he had reached the top step before the porch platform, his right foot fell right through an opening! There was no stair! He lost his balance and the grip on the basket handle; the basket's contents crashed to the pavement three floors below — splattering cans, fruit, bottles, and meats in all directions. With the assistance of the

Saint Charles parishioner, the Hometown man pulled himself to the deck of the porch and pounded on the back door of the recipient family. The suburbanite learned a sobering fact of slum life that evening. To protect themselves from predators of the night, this family removed the top step from the stairway every evening for protection. More than ever, it was apparent that there was a difference between giving a gift at the front door of a rectory and delivering that gift personally to gain a better understanding of the life that poverty imposes.

Chapter Twenty

Behind Unlocked Doors

THE STORY ABOUT THE INTRUDER horrified Pastor Kane, who was naturally concerned about the desecration of the church by a trespasser. But he was more afraid about being burglarized. There were many beautiful and expensive things in the church, like gold chalices, ciboria in the tabernacle, the six ornate golden altar candlesticks, and the vigil light box, where people deposited money to light a candle in prayer. Furthermore, by breaking into the church, a burglar could potentially find his way into the rectory, where there was a safe in a back room on the first floor holding bingo and collection money for the parish. The thought of physical assault was also threatening to Kane. My sliced black cassock showed that the neighborhood was dangerous and that an alarm wouldn't help us deal with an intruder that had already broken in.

Kane came up with a new game plan by making this beautiful church available to the community for a window of only three hours a day. Every weekday morning, the priest saying the first Mass would unlock the front east door at 6:30 A.M. for the organist and the very few parishioners who attended Mass on a daily basis. By 9:30 A.M., right after the last Mass, the church would be locked and remain so all day. Except on Tuesday. Besides it being bingo day, Pastor Kane celebrated an additional Mass at a side altar in the name of Saint Anne, the mother of Mary. Saint Anne de Beaupré is a magnificent shrine in Quebec, Canada, teeming with the constant flow of hundreds of daily pilgrims and walls cluttered with abandoned signs of healing—crutches, wheel chairs, stretchers—and filled with burning votives. On the main floor of Saint Charles, in the west transept, there was a single wooden altar, garishly painted in ivory and designated as the National Shrine of Saint Anne in the United States, very dissimilar to its counterpart in Canada. Kane and Irma sent out a bulletin to thousands of people nationally, discussing the miracles taking place at Saint Charles by the intercession of Saint Anne. With the newsletter, the cheapest religious goods were also sent as an incentive for contributions. Glow-in-the-dark rosaries, plastic holy water fonts, dashboard statues of Jesus and Mary, holy cards of Saint Anne—almost any kind of trivial religious paraphernalia that would obligate one to send a donation.

One afternoon, an old truck with Canadian plates parked alongside the iron entrance gate to the rectory. It belonged to a young couple from Ottawa with three young children who had found their way to the "National Shrine of Saint Anne in the United States," plunked in the center of Chicago's dangerous slums. Upon encountering the tightly-locked doors of the church, they rang the doorbell to the rectory, looking to visit the shrine as part of a family pilgrimage. Irma answered the door and sat the young family in the front office while she went to find the pastor. Caught totally off guard by the surprise visit, Kane wanted nothing to do with the visitors. He knew that his scam had been exposed—at least to this young family. Because he was so embarrassed, he instructed me to unlock the door to the church so that I could show them the shrine of Saint Anne. I was doing Kane's dirty work once again.

From the rectory, I took the family into the church from the side entrance and showed them the shrine. They showed me their faces of disappointment in return. There were no people, no signs of healing, not even a lit candle—just an empty church with an ugly altar devoted to Saint Anne. They looked around and asked, "Well, can we at least meet the priest that was healed?" They handed me a mimeographed sheet of paper listing me as "assistant to the shrine," explaining my eye injury, and saying that through the intercession of Saint Anne, I had been completely cured of blindness. This was a shock to me! I had nothing to do with the shrine, my vision had not been restored to what it once was, and I didn't know anything about Kane using me as a pawn to promote his ruse. The young disillusioned couple said nothing to me after I let them know in no uncertain terms that they had been misled. They asked to leave and didn't say much as I escorted them out. I was furious at Kane for letting all of this happen, especially making me experience how he had hurt these people. But Kane didn't care. Afterward, he didn't even ask anything about them. At the threat of being reprimanded, I never brought it up.

By 1959 I had served Saint Charles for more than two years, having lasted longer than my 13 predecessors who had lived with Kane beginning in 1952. It was apparent that things still weren't going well. Kane just didn't like me. He ignored my presence most of the time, and when he did speak to me, it was usually to chastise my behavior for doing things I thought a priest should do, like being friendly with the janitors and cafeteria workers in the school or getting too close to the people remaining in the parish. I couldn't figure out why he had it out for me. Maybe it was because I was Italian or because of our different philosophical points of view on how to serve the parish . . . I'm not quite sure. We just didn't get along. It bothered me, so I decided to get some advice and called an Italian priest who preceded me in serving Saint Charles—Father Len.

I knew Father Len from my grammar school days at Our Lady of the Angels. He had served under Kane at Saint Charles for one year, during which time he developed painful shingles around his abdomen, probably from nerves. Father Len was a quiet, pious man who was introspective and subscribed to the tenet of good old clerical secrecy. Even though he had known me for years, he was still hesitant in our discussion. Nevertheless, he really brought me up to speed on Kane. First, he told me not to be fooled by bingo. Kane cooked the books, not letting the archdiocese know about how much money was generated, and he kept most of it for him and Irma. The League of Saint Anne was just a scam that generated even more money for the two of them. Since Irma was the only one who handled the morning mail, no one else in the rectory had any idea of what they were pulling in. Judging by the daily mounds of returns, it was considerable.

Father Len went on to tell me about a king-sized battle that arose when Kane tried to have Irma take part in lunch and supper. As parish business was discussed during meals at the rectory table, this was Kane's way of bringing Irma into the fold. The argument ended in a screaming match where both Father Len and Father Leo threatened to take this matter to the chancery. At that last straw, Kane backed down, which only stirred Irma's ire toward the dissenting assistants.

Eventually, I asked Father Len about Muldoon. He just shut down. Seeming too frightened to talk about the rectory ghost, he did at least confirm that he knew the legends and had also experienced manifestations. But he refused to talk openly about any of it.

As we concluded our discussion, Len said something significant to me that carried me through the days ahead. “God’s grace is free. It should be made available to as many people in as many ways as possible. Father Kane is the wrong man for that place. He’s in God’s way, and there’s nothing you can do about it. So just deal with it. Believe me, you won’t get any help from downtown.”

One afternoon, it happened again. It was about 3 P.M. and the church was locked down. All entryways were locked, and the alarm in front of the tabernacle was set. Then we heard it. The steady alarm going off behind the grandfather clock made it sound as if we were in a fire station. Someone was in front of the tabernacle. At the sound of the alarm, both Bill and I rushed into the church, ready to find another intruder. But when we entered the sanctuary this time, no one was there. The alarm was still ringing frantically, but no one was standing on the altar carpet to trigger it. As we approached the tabernacle, we heard the alarm shut off from the rectory. What was going on? Was there a short in the wiring? So we tried it out. I stood on the pad, and the alarm rang; when I stepped off, the alarm shut off. Father Schumacher and I had barely locked the church again and returned to the rectory when the alarm went off once again—and then it stopped. Then on and off yet again, almost as if someone were walking back and forth in front of the main altar, stepping on the pad with each pass. We returned to the church and once again found no one there, no one hiding, no one in the empty building as the alarm went on and off another time. We locked the church and returned to the rectory once again, wondering what to fear more: the tough neighborhood or living with a ghost.

My routine on Mondays was to visit with the children in our grammar school. At 8 A.M. road barriers were placed at either end of Hoyne Avenue, creating a huge temporary play area for the hundreds of boys and girls enjoying the free time before the start of class. I would often go out to play with the children before one of the nuns rang a large hand bell to assemble the unorganized mass into disciplined lines that marched into their classrooms. Then I'd visit each classroom. Sometimes I'd stop in for a quick hello or a joke; other times I'd make up a quick story based upon a lesson from Scripture. It all depended upon the time I had available from checking on the children who didn't go to Mass the day before. Every Sunday at 9 A.M. there was a children's Mass, which was a requirement for our students. Both the children and the teachers, virtually all of them nuns, would come in and sit together. If someone missed Mass on Sunday, the nuns would know. It was my job on Mondays to follow up with those who were absent to see why they didn't make it to church.

One Monday, I spent a good part of the morning interviewing children who had missed Sunday's Mass. I must have had small conversations with at least 50 youngsters that day, three of whom gave me their Sunday contribution envelopes: one contained a penny, the second a nickel, the third was mangled and empty. I put the contents in the right-hand pocket of my cassock, intending to give this meager collection to the pastor when I returned to the rectory. But I forgot. Instead of giving the tithings directly to Kane, I left them on the top of my desk in my study, where Irma found them on Tuesday. When I wasn't in my room, she must have let herself in to snoop around, thereupon spotting the three envelopes. On Wednesday morning, Kane made a point of calling me into his office for a chat.

Filled with self-righteous indignation, the pastor asked me, "Have you been holding out on me?"

"What are you talking about?" I replied.

"The collections from the grammar school—Irma saw them on your desk. One of the envelopes was opened. How much did you take?"

I chuckled my response. "I didn't take anything. One of the kids gave me an empty envelope. There was six cents total."

"Six cents that I've caught you with," he angrily interjected. "How much more have you taken? How long has this been going on?"

"Are you serious? You think I've been stealing from the Church? This was just an honest mistake. You are blowing this way out of proportion."

Kane began shouting, "Don't you lie to me! I caught you red-handed! You'd better shape up real quick, or I'll report you to the chancery and throw you right out on your ear! You got me?"

After my scolding, I turned and left Pastor Kane's office. Irma was just outside the door, eavesdropping on my reprimand. As I passed her on the way to my room, a wry smile crossed her lips. It was now more apparent than ever that Kane was using me to show his dominance. He was showing off for Irma. I hadn't done anything wrong, yet I was in the doghouse once again. God forbid that I made a real mistake. Then I'd really be in trouble. I realized I was in quite a fragile situation with Kane, and I didn't know what to expect next. Later that night, I went to bed feeling a bit down. Of course I discussed it with Father Schumacher and Father Goedert, who encouraged me to be the best priest that I could for the parish and to not let Kane's personal differences with me get in the way. But that was easy for them to say—they were both on Kane's good side. They didn't have to deal with the accusations and the berating—I did. And it was taking its toll on my self-confidence and on my lifelong ambition of being a priest. As I realized that there was nothing I could do about Kane that night, I went to bed and figured I'd try to start fresh the following morning.

On this night, as every night, I locked my bedroom door—an oversized thick oak door. Per my usual routine, I left the skeleton key in the keyhole so I wouldn't lose it. Another reason for leaving it there was so nobody else could use a different skeleton key to enter my room in the middle of the night.

At about three in the morning, something drew me out of my deep sleep. Still in bed, I slowly opened my eyes to find my bedroom door wide open, with the skeleton key firmly set in the keyhole. Though startled, I laid there for a moment longer while I tried to figure out what was going on. From the hallway, a soft beam of intense light infused my room and was bathing my face, which is probably what woke me up in the first place. It was coming from the lamp keeping vigil to Muldoon's painting on the wall in the corridor. As I assessed the situation from my bed, my eyes came into contact with the portrait of Muldoon, almost as if I was seeing a ghost face to face. I was spooked. Never mind the fact that my door had mysteriously opened, but that my waking moment in the middle of the night was looking right at Muldoon was enough to give any unbeliever the creeps. Sitting up at the edge of my bed, I continued to just look at Muldoon—it seemed almost as if he was trying to tell me something. It might sound foolish, but from my bedside I looked that portrait straight in the eye and said aloud, "Look, Muldoon, I'm a good guy. Don't bug me. I'm on your side." With that, I got up, locked the door, and slowly fell back to sleep. The next morning at the breakfast table, Father Schumacher was amazed at my story.

I experienced the exact same incident less than a month later.

Unlocking Pandora's Box. (Illustration by David Facchini.)

∞

In the midst of the dismal happenings in our neighborhood and rectory life, the legend of Muldoon was a pleasant distraction to Father Schumacher, Father Goedert, and me. Upon greeting each other, we would usually quip, "Anything up with Muldoon lately?" For us, the legend was like a snowball rolling downhill, becoming larger with every passing manifestation. Through years of living together, Father Schumacher and I surmised that the ghost of Muldoon wasn't a maniacal spirit. He didn't seem to do anything harmful, at least not to us. It seemed as if there was some correlation between what we believed were Muldoon hauntings and the unfortunate turn of events of the parish under the reign of Pastor Kane. Over time, Bill and I came to the conclusion that Muldoon was acting as our guide in serving the parish of Saint Charles. Our belief was that when the parish strayed from its mission, Muldoon made himself known.

Chapter Twenty-one

Obedience, the Holiest Virtue

THE CATHOLIC CHURCH HAS tolerated many abuses from its priests, such as drunkenness and immorality. These are emotional sins where the flesh is weak and a man can get caught in the heat of the moment. The one thing the Church will not tolerate is sin of the intellect, such as insubordination. The intellect is a person's highest faculty, the conscious mind at work. A sin of the intellect is committed knowingly and willingly, and when that sin is against the Church, it signifies rejection. It is inexcusable.

Back in the seminary, a bell called Vox Dei (the Voice of God) regulated all of the day's activities, from reveille at 5:25 A.M. to lights out at 9:45 P.M. The bell signified our response to God, which was more meritorious when made with haste. Like Pavlov's dog, a seminarian was conditioned to respond immediately to the Vox Dei. If he was writing a paper in his room when the bell rang, he should put his pencil down immediately, even if in midsentence, and move on to the next assignment of the day. Our obedience was modeled after the Passion of Christ. When standing in judgment before Pilate, Jesus was urged to offer some kind of defense, but instead said nothing. In Latin, Scripture says, *Jesus autem tacevit* (Jesus was silent). In the imitation of Christ, seminarians were conditioned to obey silently and without resistance. By the time I was ordained, my class marched in lockstep, like robots trained to new assignments in strictest obedience, no longer to the Vox Dei, but to the every whim of the pastor. It was this obedience that kept me loyal to Pastor Kane of Saint Charles for more than three years.

A change was about to take place in me that would alter my future life as a priest. It was the early winter of 1959. Tuesday again—another day set aside for bingo. Bill Schumacher prepared the jar game and stacked the prize booth with scores of dolls, toasters, and radios. Pastor Kane slept in, as he did most Tuesdays, to prepare himself for the important day that lay ahead of him. I set out the bingo cards and the record sheets first thing in the morning to help free up the rest of my day. After saying Mass that morning, I was told by the cook that a woman asking for "Father Fettuccini" had come to the rectory and was waiting for me in the front office. When I entered the room, a black, matronly woman tearfully asked if I would help bury her seven-year-old son, who had died suddenly from an unidentified illness. I had seen this woman before. She and her only son were not Catholics but had come to Sunday Mass often, and I knew the boy had expressed the desire to come to our parochial school. The woman went on to say that her son was laid out in a small black funeral parlor on Roosevelt Road just east of Ashland. Of all the days of the week that she needed my help, with my luck, it had to be on a Tuesday. By now it was still quite early in the morning, only 9 A.M. Because I had already set up bingo, I figured that if I left right away, I would be back home before 11. That left me plenty of time to do whatever else still needed to be done. Besides, these people had come to me for help in their grieving. How could I say no?

Irma was in the kitchen. When I came out of the office, I told her to let Pastor Kane know I had set up bingo and needed to attend to this unexpected request; I shouldn't be too long. But it was winter and I had to walk. Though I had prepared myself for the cold by wearing my black coat and leather gloves, the unshoveled snow of about six inches that crunched under my galoshes slowed my progress much more than I had anticipated. I had to walk a mile to my destination. Not one stretch of sidewalk was shoveled in this neighborhood.

As I entered the small funeral parlor, I could see the puzzlement on the black undertaker's face. I don't think he had ever seen a white priest conduct a funeral service in his establishment before. He brought me to the boy's mother, who sat in a rocking chair before the small closed coffin, and introduced me to the grieving friends of this small family. To console them, I spoke from the heart about how Jesus loved little children. I can't remember everything I said to the brokenhearted mother that morning, but I remember that my talk was constantly interrupted with "Amen," which I wasn't accustomed to. After the small service, the mother kissed my right cheek to thank me. This was the boy's only service. From there, he was taken directly to the cemetery to be buried. As I left, the funeral director, who was so reserved when I walked into the parlor, came from behind a pillar and approached me with a handshake and a friendly good-bye. I walked out the door knowing that I had done the work of God that day, the kind of work for which I went into the seminary to begin with.

Struggling against the strong wind blowing from the west wasn't my only concern as I walked back to the rectory. Even though the cold air was filled with stinging ice pellets that hit my face, my biggest concern was Kane. I knew I would have to pay a price for leaving the rectory on a Tuesday morning. As I trudged home, I was filled with anxiety and dread. Even though deep down I knew that I had done the right thing, I also knew that as soon as I walked through the door, Kane was going to attack me for my unspeakable act of abandonment on bingo day. He was going to let me have it. I nervously went through the iron gate leading to the front porch, and with frozen fingers, I unlocked the front door. The thick oak door seemed heavier than ever before, almost as if it were trying to resist my entry to the rectory, as if the door were trying to protect me from what lay ahead. As I entered, Pastor Kane was standing outside the door of the main office, just as I had anticipated. He was furious. Kane must have pent up all of his aggravation while I was gone, as he seemed ready to explode. "Where have you been all this time?" he screamed, invading every corner of the building with his angry voice. "Get in here!" he shouted, as he pointed to one of the front offices. "We're going to get some things straight!"

Catching a gloating smile on Irma's face for the verbal assault I was about to get, I walked into the room with my tail between my legs. The irate pastor was right behind me, slamming the office door so fiercely behind us, the windows rattled and the pictures on the walls shook. I stood there, trying to plead my case: to let Pastor Kane know that while he was asleep, a grieving woman came to the rectory asking me to pray over her son's modest funeral; to let him know that my bingo preparation had already been completed; to let him know that I had asked Irma to tell him that I would be back by 11 A.M., which I was. But Kane was too angry to hear me. He wasn't about to accept anything I said.

"This woman . . . was she Catholic?" Kane demanded to know.

"No, but what difference does it make!"

"What difference does it make?" Kane got right in my face. Nose to nose, he exclaimed, "Do you know who I am?"

I remained silent.

In a stronger and more strident pitch, Kane screamed, "Do you know who you are?" He cussed at me, using every profanity you could think of, spraying my face with his spittle as he bawled me out. He went on and on and on—and I just remained silent, almost catatonic. I looked firmly through his gold-rim eyeglasses into his unmerciful eyes, and for the first time, I noticed that he had no eyelashes. I focused on his bulbous nose, only inches from mine, and on his cheeks, which were badly pockmarked, like the rough skin of a pineapple, and on his complexion, which grew redder and redder as he yelled. I focused on anything that would keep me from hearing his words and feeling his rage.

"Did you learn anything in the seminary? What I say goes! You got that? You're just a punk and a crummy priest. Without me, you'd be out on the street. You'd better learn something awfully quick. I'm the boss around here, damn it! I call the shots! You got that?"

I got it, all right. And with that my dago got the best of me. I lost my temper and finally let him have it.

"You wanna fight, Kane? Okay, you've got one! You think I'm such a crummy priest? Let's call the chancery. I've got plenty to tell them! I know all your tricks. I've learned all your secrets. Why don't we talk about you and Irma? Or better yet, we could talk about how you're running this place into the ground. Or would you rather I tell them about stealing from bingo and the League of Saint Anne? Come on, Kane, let's go downtown and see what they have to say about all of this!"

My rebellion wasn't something that Pastor Kane was expecting, and like any bully, he immediately backed down. Almost instantly, Kane quieted and regained his composure. His face drooped and his smug and vengeful posture grew limp. He stepped away from me, immediately changing his entire demeanor and tried to calm me down. "Okay, calm down now . . . let's both calm down." He collapsed right in front of me like a house of cards. "We don't need to tell anyone else in the house about this. This is between just you and me, okay?"

Making up for all the years of pent-up anger, I kept at him. All my training in strict obedience went right out the window. "You want to see a crummy priest, look in the mirror. You are a mean bastard. I'm tired of doing your dirty work. You don't do anything around here but hide and count your bingo money, and meanwhile the whole parish is going to pot. There are people in this neighborhood who need our help, and I'll be damned if I'm not going to at least try to give them a hand."

Kane was silent. He had exhausted himself yelling at me, was surprised by my retaliation, and knew he had no defense to argue with me any further. During the heat of my tirade, the pastor hung his head in defeat, opened the door, walked through the rectory and up the stairway to his room, and locked the door behind him. When I came out of the office, Irma and the cook stood gaping at me, having overheard our fight. Irma harrumphed out of the room, and the cook returned to preparing lunch, while I stood in the entrance of the office battleground in silent victory.

Coincidentally, Cardinal Meyer put an official end to bingo in archdiocesan parishes by the end of the year. Although my battle was over, the cold war in the rectory grew icier and stronger. It was Kane and Irma against me. Their indifference toward me grew through exclusion. They stopped telling me about functions so that my absence would make me look bad to parishioners. They ignored me in the rectory as if I didn't exist. And behind my back, both Kane and Irma bad-mouthed me to Father Schumacher, trying to turn Bill against me as well. Because I had told Kane and

Irma that I had figured them out, they were making my life more miserable at Saint Charles than ever. They wanted me out. Like the number of priests before me who worked under Kane, I realized that I had reached the end of the line in this parish. I also recognized that for three years, I had given Pastor Kane the power to be my judge. I was different now. I had taken his power away. I vowed to never again let someone else dictate who I was going to be. My newfound independence provided me with the opportunity to redefine what I wanted to accomplish as a priest. I wanted to serve an Italian community. Kane's request for an Italian priest, whose cultural background and bilingual skills were no longer needed in this community, had detoured me from that dream long enough. Either because of inattention or the ineffective distribution of Italian priests, the Italians in the archdiocese were poorly served. I knew that there was a place where I really belonged, and my goal was to get back on track.

Doing some research and utilizing Bill Schumacher's typing skills, I wrote a letter to the vicar general, Monsignor George Casey, with the intent of meeting Albert Cardinal Meyer to discuss how the archdiocese could use its few Italian-American priests to a greater advantage. Within several days of receiving my letter, I was called to a private conference with the cardinal. Our one-on-one conversation was quiet and brief. Cardinal Meyer was aware that Italian priests were not being well utilized by the archdiocese and agreed that some reassignments would do some good. Then he asked me which parishes had a large Italian congregation and could use an Italian-speaking priest. I named seven. By the following spring, Cardinal Meyer had appointed other Italian priests to six of the parishes I mentioned. In 1960 I was sent to the seventh, Saint John Bosco at Grand and Austin. My days at Saint Charles were through.

∞

It was not an easy decision for me to leave the parish of Saint Charles Borromeo. By that time, I had established a strong presence with the few people in the community and the children and nuns at the parochial school, and I had built significant friendships with Father Schumacher and Father Goedert. I knew that by requesting a transfer, I was leaving behind everything that I had worked for during the past four years.

My last day at Saint Charles Borromeo was much like my first. I left without ceremony and with little acknowledgment. My brother picked me up in the same tan Chevy beater. I didn't have much more stuff, maybe a few additional boxes of books and such. Leaving was like a matching bookend to the volumes of my first four years of experience as a priest: adventures on the harsh Chicago streets, odd rectory incidents, learning to stand up for myself, and the establishment of relationships with Father Goedert, Father Schumacher, and the rectory ghost.

Chapter Twenty-two

The *Days* to Demolition

BY OCTOBER OF 1961, PASTOR Kane was reappointed to a parish on Chicago's North Side. Of course Duke and Irma loyally accompanied him to his new parish. Father Pat Navin replaced Pastor Kane later that same month. Pastor Navin was not what you would consider an orthodox priest. He was well known throughout Chicago for his crass demeanor. To hear him talk, you would think he was a construction worker rather than a man of the cloth. He cussed, he was boorish, and, surprisingly, he was the best thing that had happened to the parish for about a decade. Navin's tough exterior matched the tough neighborhood that encapsulated Saint Charles. He often said that he belonged in this small community of the poor and crude. Yet despite his gruffness, he was a man of good heart and he endeared himself to the parish. He treated the priests of the house fairly and with decency, something Kane was never able to do. He brought a renewed spirit to the parish and to rectory life at Saint Charles. He fit in well.

Navin was very familiar with the life of Bishop Muldoon. He grew up in the parish of Holy Name Cathedral and had direct knowledge of Bishop Muldoon's controversy with Jeremiah J. Crowley. In fact, as children, he and his sister attended the Mass that was shut down by the presence of the excommunicated Crowley. Pastor Navin was also familiar with the legend of Muldoon's ghost. He had heard stories through the grapevine. When Navin arrived at Saint Charles, Father Schumacher, who continued for two years as Navin's assistant, briefed him with our ghost stories. Navin took a hard-line approach with the ghost of Muldoon. Jerry Maloney, who followed me at Saint Charles, recounts that Navin's first act was to relocate the painting that Kane hung in appeasement on the second floor. Instead of having it outside the pastor's quarters, Navin moved it to a dark wall outside the first-floor dining room above a metal radiator. Hung without illumination, the painting was respectfully displayed, though not as a shrine, as Kane had erected, inhibiting the daily lives of everyone living in the rectory. Make no mistake—Pastor Navin believed in the ghost of Muldoon; he just wanted no part of him. Upon the painting's rehanging, Maloney recalls how Navin stood right in front of the portrait. Pointing his right forefinger into its face, the pastor sternly issued an ultimatum: "Muldoon, you screw with me and you're goin' right out onto Roosevelt Road!"

With the coming of Navin, many clergy familiar with the legend maintain that the Muldoon manifestations stopped. Some say that Navin's obscene language and rough demeanor scared off the bishop's gentle ghost. But I can say that isn't entirely true. At least when I returned to the parish, Muldoon made himself known once again. It was December 1961, and I had been serving the parish of Saint John Bosco for more than a year. I kept in touch with Father Schumacher from time to time and knew that the poor people of Saint Charles could use all the help they could get, especially during the cold Christmas holiday. Through the Legion of Mary, I organized a modest Advent clothing drive to provide some help.

Having been a priest for five years, I was able to purchase my first car, a gray anthracite Volkswagen Beetle, for $1,800—brand new. But it didn't have a heater; instead, the heat was generated by the engine's manifold, and it took driving a couple of miles to get any heat from the darn thing. With the first of two carloads of clothes for the needy of my old parish piled high in my back seat, I drove down to the rough side of town with one of the youngest members of the Legion of Mary to help me with the delivery. Tim, a young high school student in his first or second year at Steinmetz High School, was interested in accompanying me on my Christmas mission. I appreciated the companionship and needed the help to carry these items into the rectory. It was evening, and as we pulled up, Bill Schumacher was waiting for us at the rectory door. After we unloaded our Christmas cargo, my young helper asked to use the bathroom and I directed him to a small washroom under the impressive wood stairway leading to the priests' quarters on the second floor. Meanwhile, I ran upstairs for a quick chat with Father Schumacher. After my brief visit, I went back down to find Tim waiting for me in the foyer at the foot of the stairs. All the lights in the working office were burning brightly, though I remembered it being dark and empty when I had gone upstairs.

On the way back home, Tim asked me, "Who was that nice old priest in the office?"

"What old priest?" I asked, knowing that the only priests in the rectory that night were Bill and myself.

"The priest in the office with all the lights on . . . near the bathroom."

"What did he look like?"

"He was older, a bit heavy, with a roundish face. I said hello to him and he just smiled back."

From what Tim was describing, I didn't know of any priest in the house that matched that description. I kind of brushed his comment off and switched the topic of conversation. Two weeks later, Tim and I returned to Saint Charles with another carload for the poor. This time, we arrived during the winter dusk of late afternoon, and the main floor of the rectory was well lit. Father Schumacher asked us to carry the items up to his room, where he would sort them out for the Saint Vincent DePaul Society. As we carried the bundles upstairs to his room, Tim noticed the painting of Muldoon. He stopped, dropped his packages, and pointed to the portrait and shouted to me, "Father, that's him. That's the priest I saw last time. Who is he?" I didn't say a thing. Father Schumacher, who was helping us with the packages, too, stood in awe. During our ride home, I composed myself and for the first time began telling the legend of Muldoon to my young friend. He had seen a ghost.

Father Schumacher went on to serve Saint Charles Borromeo for seven years before being relocated to a parish in the northwest suburbs of Chicago. We kept in touch from time to time, remaining good friends. But staying in touch is never the same as the friendship that you experience by living day in and day out with someone. Whenever we got together, we would discuss the "good" old days at Saint Charles and laughed at how miserable Pastor Kane made our lives. And no matter what, our conversations always led back to Muldoon. This was the case when both Bill and I returned to Saint Charles to attend one of the last confirmations for the grammar school children of the parish. As is common when a bunch of priests gather at these functions, there were about six of us standing around in the old rectory that Gill built, discussing how things were going for the parish. Eventually, Bill asked, "So what's new with Muldoon?" Father Schumacher's successor, Father Jack, told another unnerving tale.

Reconstructed by Samuel Cardinal Stritch, Holy Trinity Parish remained to serve the rising needs of the West Side Medical Center. (Photo by David Facchini and Marko Kevo.)

It was a Sunday night, and Father Jack was the only priest in the rectory that evening waiting for his brother and sister-in-law to pick him up for a steak dinner at a restaurant on Wabash Avenue. When his family arrived, the three of them enjoyed a drink in the priest's room before leaving. The sister-in-law asked to use the washroom, and Father Jack showed her where it was—down the corridor and next to the small room at the back of the rectory. Once at the restaurant, Father Jack's sister-in-law asked, "Who was that nice old priest in the room next to the bathroom?" Father Jack was puzzled. Apparently, when his sister-in-law came out of the bathroom, she noticed lights coming from the room at the back of the rectory. She stepped to the doorway of the back room to say hello, and there was a pleasant old priest sitting in the chair next to the bed. She waved and said hello to him, and he just smiled. Father Jack could think of only one priest it could have been that evening. It had to have been Muldoon, sitting in one of his favorite places, the single room at the back of the rectory.

By the mid-1960s, there was not much life left to my former parish. Almost in direct correlation, as Saint Charles Borromeo dwindled, Holy Trinity grew. As a result of Pastor Kane's rejection of a hospital ministry years prior, Cardinal Stritch redeveloped Holy Trinity into the parish of the West Side Medical Center. In 1966, as the grammar school at Saint Charles closed its doors, the old German church at Taylor and Wolcott was leveled. A new combination church and school for the parish of Holy Trinity was erected and dedicated by John Cardinal Cody on October 28, 1967. After the closing of the school, the demise of the rest of Saint Charles was not far behind. There were few people left to serve, and keeping the parish's doors open no longer made any sense. On February 2, 1968, Saint Charles was officially consolidated with Holy Trinity. The few families left were transferred to Holy Trinity, and all of the school, baptismal, and marriage records were shipped to Taylor Street. Pastor Navin remained by himself at Saint Charles until November 28, 1968, when the entire complex—church, rectory, convent, and school—was closed down and placed under the jurisdiction of the pastor of Holy Trinity, Father John Marren.

The final days of Saint Charles were grim. Living blocks away and without protective resources, Father Marren was unable to guard the Saint Charles complex from thievery and gross abuse. The church, rectory, convent, and school were methodically picked apart by pillagers, stone-by-stone, piece-by-piece, bit-by-bit. Father Schumacher and Father Goedert said they stopped by from time to time during those final days before demolition. Ray remembers driving by the deserted convent, seeing the double doors wide open, the entrance walls stripped of the marble wall tiles, and the once fine lace curtains, now weathered and torn, draped out of shattered windows. Bill told me of going into the church to find empty beer and whiskey bottles and used condoms lying around the main altar. Everything that was of any value at the complex that was thoughtfully constructed by Muldoon decades before was stripped from the church, school, and rectory: toilets, doorknobs, desks, faucets, sinks. If the object could bring even the smallest price, it was taken. Statues, stained glass—you name it. Even some pews were ripped up from the floor and moved right out the door. To this day, no one can figure out why someone didn't step in to salvage the valuables of the church. Of it all, the one thing Father Schumacher was able to rescue was one of the six large golden candlesticks that had graced the main altar.

By the power of eminent domain, the archdiocese sold the parish complex to Cook County in order to make way for bigger and better things. After 1968 giant bulldozers and big metal wrecking balls demolished the church's mighty stone walls, which were as much as two feet thick and built to last for centuries. Within a short time, there was no trace left of Saint Charles. It was as if the parish never existed. Known to few today, it has become a forgotten parish.

∞

To my knowledge, the two episodes just recounted are the only two times Muldoon made himself visually known to anyone. Both of the people who experienced these manifestations firsthand have asked to remain anonymous. I can respect that. Father Jack is now a retired priest in poor health. The last thing he needs is to be bombarded with questions about seeing a ghost. As for Tim, he went on to become a priest and is prominent in his diocese in Chicago's suburbs. We continue to remain good friends to this day and usually get together every Christmas to have dinner and to catch up with each other. In 1999, when I mentioned to him that I was planning to write a book about Muldoon, Father Tim replied, "Well, I hope that you're going to include the story of when I saw him." I had totally forgotten about it. After we discussed it for a little bit, and he jogged my memory about the haunting, I asked him if he was sure about seeing Muldoon. A bit peeved at my doubting remarks, Tim said, "Rock, I know what I saw! I saw Muldoon! I saw him as clearly as I see you now!" He, too, didn't want curious people continually asking him about seeing a ghost. As a man who respects his privacy and has kept the story of Muldoon quiet for almost 40 years, I can't say that I blame him.

Chapter Twenty-three

Living with a Ghost

TODAY, THE PARISH OF SAINT Charles Borromeo is a fading memory. There are no signs that there was once a church that stood proudly at the corner of Roosevelt and Hoyne—in a region that Native American peoples once revered as sacred; in the vicinity where Marquette first evangelized the Gospel of Christ; at the location where Henneberry and Gill started a huge and vibrant parish based upon Damen's premise of parochial education; at the exact place where Muldoon built a magnificent set of ecclesiastical buildings for the greater glory of God. At the intersection, there are no markers or plaques dedicated to buildings built to last for centuries that were prematurely laid to rest after a brief 84-year time span. The corner that was once holy ground is now home to a multi-tiered parking garage for the Juvenile Court of Cook County. Today, Holy Trinity, still at Taylor and Wolcott, continues to serve Chicago's West Side Medical Center, which is

A six-story parking garage for the Cook County Juvenile Court now stands at the former site of St. Charles Borromeo at Roosevelt Road and Hoyne Avenue. (Photo by David Facchini and Marko Kevo.)

now, perhaps, the world's largest complex for patient care and medical studies. The parish embraces Cook County (Stroger) Hospital, the University of Illinois Hospital, Rush-Presbyterian-Saint Luke's Hospital, the West Side Veterans Hospital, and many other medical and higher education institutions in the area. If Kane would have been willing to undertake hospital ministry, the success of Holy Trinity parish could have easily been that of Saint Charles Borromeo.

After Saint Charles, Pastor Kane went with Irma and Duke to a blue-collar parish on Chicago's North Side. Just as before, Kane was said to still be an unpleasant person to live with, and the ever-present Irma continued to be a problem for other priests living in the rectory. She kept interfering with church business and made the work of the assistants nearly impossible. After a short stay, Kane was transferred to work in a parish in the northwestern suburbs, from where he eventually retired. The trio then moved to the West Coast, where, in retirement, Kane worked as a chaplain for a military school (in California). Somewhere along the line, Kane wrote a book about his best friend, Duke, comparing the mutt to the Holy Spirit and writing Lassie-like accolades about the dog. Duke eventually died, and Kane and Irma returned to the Chicago area, living in a condo in Park Ridge. Pastor Kane died in the late 1980s and was buried as pastor emeritus from the last parish that he served in the Chicago Archdiocese. I heard that, at the funeral, Irma sat alone at the front of the church in the family pew.

In 1963 Father Schumacher was transferred to Saint Cyprian's in River Grove, Illinois. Eventually, the archdiocese let his light shine, appointing him to the Archdiocesan Matrimonial Tribunal in the Chancery Office and giving him residency at Saint Andrew's near Wrigley Field. Bill went on to astonish everyone with his intellectual brilliance and the newfound compassion and understanding he had developed through many years of slum ministry. Father Goedert also did quite well for himself in the archdiocese. Ray continued on at Saint Charles longer than both of us and was eventually transferred to Blessed Sacrament Parish on Chicago's Near West Side. He served as a resident of a suburban parish until he was appointed pastor of Saint Barnabas on the South Side of Chicago. In the footsteps of Muldoon, he was eventually consecrated auxiliary bishop (on August 12, 1991) and was made vicar general during the last days of one of Chicago's most celebrated archbishops—an Italian, nonetheless—Joseph Cardinal Bernardin. After Bernardin died, Bishop Goedert became administrator of the archdiocese for many months, until the appointment the city's new archbishop, Francis Cardinal George.

As for me, I served the parish of Saint John Bosco until 1966, when I was transferred to the thriving parish of Our Lady, Help of Christians. But by then, and despite all the revisions decreed by Pope John XXIII through the Second Vatican Council in 1965, I had already made my decision to leave the priesthood. As Saint Thomas Aquinas once put it, in order to achieve fulfillment, a person has to work to his or her potential. For many reasons, I never felt that I had that opportunity as a priest. I finalized my intention of leaving active ministry through John Cardinal Cody in March 1971. At a meeting in his mansion on State Parkway, I told Cardinal Cody of my intentions. He was kind and gracious, even offering me my own parish if I continued as a priest. But my mind was made up—it was time to go. Before I left his office that day, Cardinal Cody gave a grave warning about leaving. He told me that I would not readily find a job, that my parents, friends, and the Italian community in general would reject me. I'd be an outcast to the priests I once knew as my friends and colleagues. I would have nothing and have to start building a new life for myself from scratch. I don't know where he got these insights, but his predictions never came true.

After officially leaving the priesthood, I was immediately hired by Carl DeMoon, a former Scalabrinian priest from Our Lady of the Angels who had started his own real estate company. I began by overseeing his five offices located in the western suburbs and eventually became a real estate broker. Within a year I took a position with the Wirtz Realty Corporation as a residential property manager, where I remained for 27 years. In a strange coincidence, one of the residents of a building that I managed, at 2970 N. Sheridan Road, was the last pastor of Saint Charles Borromeo, Father Pat Navin, who lived by himself in retirement in Lakeview. Father Navin eventually lost his right foot to diabetes before dying in 1985.

In 1972 I married Della and we had two boys. The years passed quickly. From time to time, we'd have Father Schumacher and Father Goedert over for dinner. In 1993 they both visited my home together for the last time. Bill had developed incurable lung cancer and was about to announce his retirement from the chancery. He wanted to spend his last days in Santa Fe, New Mexico, a place where Bill felt that he had a strong link to his father, who worked as an executive for the Santa Fe Railroad. That last night together, the three of us reminisced and laughed about Kane and all the craziness at Saint Charles, and of course we talked about Muldoon. Later in the evening, Bill mentioned that he was leaving to me in his will the one item he had salvaged from Saint Charles, the ornate golden candlestick from the main altar. He told me the surviving candlestick sat in his library at St. Andrew's rectory, and he wanted me to have it as a remembrance of our friendship, our work together at Saint Charles, and our experiences with the ghost of Muldoon.

(From left to right) Schumacher, Facchini, and Goedert, reunited at Father Schumacher's retirement party. (Photo from the Facchini family collection.)

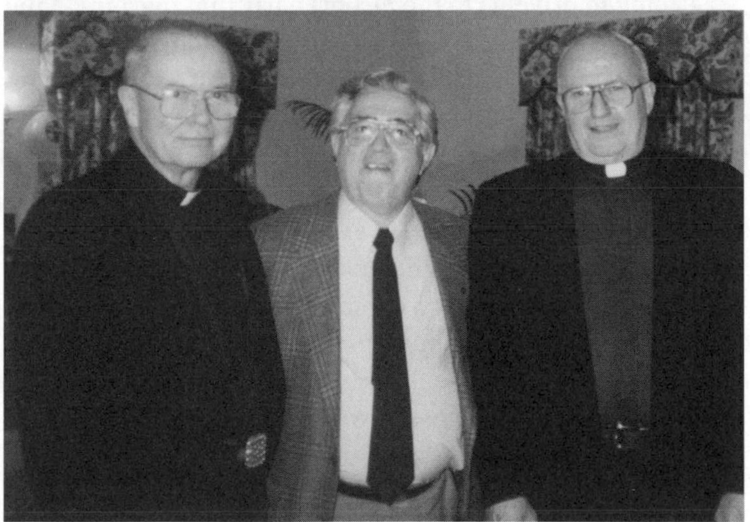

Father William Allen Schumacher died on November 29, 1994, at the age of 66. As Bill was an official of the chancery, Cardinal Bernardin presided at his funeral in the presence of all Chicago's auxiliary bishops at Saint Andrew's Church. Bishop Goedert preached one of his finest sermons—a tribute to an intellectual's humanity. In a strange parallel, much like Muldoon's episcopal ring that never made it back to Saint Charles, I never received that candlestick. Today, in my small library, next to the black binder of philosophy notes that Bill penned years ago in the seminary, I have an invaluable book that serves as a remembrance of our friendship: Father Schumacher's doctoral dissertation in which he signed "To Father Rocco Facchini: my companion in preaching the Gospel to the poor."

April 17, 2001—my wife and I and two close friends had scheduled a ten-day trip to California. To cap off my book, I wanted to visit Muldoon's birthplace in Columbia and his boyhood town of Stockton. As travel is more involved for a dialysis patient, my wife worked hard in setting up dialysis appointments for our stays in Eureka and Fremont. We were scheduled to leave for San Francisco at 8:40 A.M., and my son was going to drive us to the airport early that morning. I felt fine. My bags were packed and we were ready to go, when all of a sudden my head was swirling. The next thing I knew, David was calling into my face. Della called the paramedics, and I was immediately whisked off to Swedish Covenant Hospital for my fifth hospitalization within a year. The emergency crew worked intensely over me, and I was subjected to every bodily invasion imaginable.

After some hours, my condition stabilized and I found myself alone in a darkened emergency room. I was disoriented and uncomfortable. I was on oxygen and an IV and had been poked with needles. It was an awful feeling—sadly, one that I have grown much too accustomed to. But as I lay there in the quiet, I looked beyond my feet to the dark background of the room and wondered if I was going to make it through to finish this book. I asked out loud, "Muldoon, am I going to get this book done?" Within minutes, my anxiety and bodily discomfort melted away, and I felt a serenity that I had not felt before. Somehow, I knew that I would finish. Despite being in the hospital time and again since then, I guess I got it done.

Looking back on a lifetime of living with the legend of Muldoon, I've always been conscious of his presence, not knowing how or when he would manifest himself. Not really knowing why, either. As a young assistant at Saint Charles, I felt Muldoon would make himself known late at night to protest the pastor's lack of ministry in the parish. After Saint Charles was destroyed, I came to realize that Muldoon was trying to warn us about the impending demolition of the church he had so lovingly built. Today, through researching his life and the Crowley scandal and through writing this book, I wonder if he made himself known to me as a way to help vindicate his tarnished reputation. With faith, I believe that everything happens for a reason. So maybe long before I even realized it, Muldoon chose me to write this book to help set his spirit free. Perhaps Muldoon was always meant to be part of my destiny from the day I set foot in Saint Charles: The serendipity throughout my life regarding Muldoon had an objective. My fate was to write a book about my first four years as a priest, which I had kept to myself for decades. All that being said, writing this book has given me purpose as well. It has carried me through years of illness and has allowed me to reminisce and to share and to build something with my family and friends. I've even thought of writing another book . . . maybe one of these days.

∞

On Saturday, August 3, 2002, my son Dan and I were putting the finishing touches on this final chapter. We climbed the stairway up to the spare bedroom where we had spent weekend upon weekend writing and editing what you have just read. Before we got started, Dan went to the bathroom, and about four hours later, he used it once again. From the washroom, he called downstairs to his wife, "Hey, Jodi, did you turn this radio on in here?" Dan knew the radio was not on before, and no one had been in the washroom since. As the two of them tried to figure it out, I began laughing to myself. It was just the kind of thing that Muldoon was famous for. Perhaps this was his playful stamp of approval on our hard work. It seemed to me that Muldoon was up to his old tricks once again.

EPILOGUE

by Sharon Woodhouse, publisher of Lake Claremont Press

DID THE GHOST OF MULDOON *fade away with the demolition of St. Charles Borromeo?* In 2001 I received a book proposal from Rocco Facchini saying that our company was recommended to him by a mutual colleague who thought our Chicago specialty, including books on the history behind local ghostlore, might be a good match for his Muldoon project. Though I hadn't seen or heard the name "Facchini" in years, I knew right away that this wasn't my only link to Rocco. Rocco's wife Della had stood up in my parents' wedding when she and they worked at Victor Adding Machine together. I had never met Rocco, but I remembered my parents telling me that Della had married an ex-priest. I smiled at the coincidence and wondered if Rocco realized that I was Pat and Woody's daughter, but didn't read further than the introduction.

A couple days later, immediately after I went to bed, someone began pacing outside my door, making the floor boards creak. Two steps this way. Two steps that way. I sat up and noticed that there was no light coming in under the door from the kitchen. *Why is my roommate pacing so close in front of my door and not going anywhere else?* I thought, kind of annoyed. After more than 45 minutes of pacing, I must have fallen asleep. I awoke around 3:30 A.M. to more of the same pacing, but this time my heart was pounding. *What's going on?* This certainly wasn't my roommate, and it's not likely an intruder—the footsteps aren't going anywhere! It was almost another 45 minutes of sitting up staring at the door, listening and trying to determine what was going on, before I got out of bed to confront what was out there. Nothing, of course. I paced back and forth in front of my room, re-creating the sounds I had heard, and investigated other possible causes, eventually going back to sleep stumped. After relaying the odd experience to a few people the next day, it occurred to me that I hadn't read more about the ghostly Muldoon, and I rifled through my pile in search of Rocco's proposal.

A few weeks later I had dinner with the Facchini family to talk about the possibility of Lake Claremont Press publishing Rocco's book. Included in Rocco's stories of St. Charles Borromeo was the detail that others' first experience with the ghost of Muldoon was often his pacing outside their doors!

One afternoon several weeks after that, I was at my desk when I became aware that someone was hanging over my shoulder, more than a little too close for comfort. Karen Formanski was the only other person in the office that day, and I wondered without looking around, *Why is she so close?* I decided to ignore it, but felt a growing discomfort. *Even if she were using my printer, why is she so much in my space?* As I tried to discreetly look behind me to see just how close she was and why, the back of my chair was kicked and I lurched forward into the desk. That's when I turned around completely and saw that Karen was nowhere near me. She was in the back of the office on the phone, where she had been for quite a while.

I hadn't yet sent Rocco a contract to review. Somehow, this nudge from nowhere jolted my memory of that, and I took care of it within the week.

There was another day when some friends and I were settled in my kitchen, talking about our work and current projects. The conversation eventually came around to Muldoon and whether or not I was going to publish it. To liven up my dry work tales, I mentioned, as an aside, the pacing and kicked chair incidents. No sooner did the stories get out of my mouth, when the CD tower in the living room toppled, with no discernible provocation, spilling discs across the room.

Still later, before we had finished negotiating the contract, I was in New York City making plans with a publishing friend for an after-work drink. He suggested an Irish bar on the corner near his office, but couldn't remember its name. When I arrived at Third Avenue and 43rd Street, I saw the name on the awning that I wouldn't forget: MULDOON'S. "So what are you going to publish next?" he asked.

Soon after that, the Facchinis and I agreed on a contract.

Fast forward to the day in December 2002 when Dan Facchini was scheduled to drop off the finished manuscript. I was awakened from a deep sleep at 5 A.M. by what sounded like a blaring choir outside my room. I opened my door and stepped into my kitchen, which was resounding with an almost deafening version of *O Holy Night*. I was the only one home. There turned out to be a Christmas album in my CD player, but *Why was it on?* and *How did it get to be so outrageously loud?*

There are a number of rationalizations for these seeming coincidences and "unexplainable" occurrences, but regardless of their source, they did seem to happen in conjunction with specific steps of the book publishing process, particularly at the moments when I wavered or set it aside.

Perhaps ghosts are real manifestations from other dimensions. I'm more inclined to consider them as metaphors for the things that continue to haunt us, or the ephemera that creep under our skin and influence our choices. Whatever the case, it's apparent to me that early on, I must have joined Rocco Facchini and his family and tuned in to the spirit of Muldoon.

∞

Shortly before Muldoon went to press, Rocco and Della stopped in our office to drop off some photos. She relayed an incident that happened to her a few days earlier. She was driving with several friends in her car, and one asked how Rock's book was coming along. As Della was bringing everyone up to date, she didn't realize how close she was coming to the car in front of her until she had to stop suddenly to avoid hitting it. Her eyes then found its license plate: M-U-L-D-O-O-N.

Chicago-Area Churches Blessed or Dedicated by Auxiliary Bishop Peter J. Muldoon from 1901 to 1907

1. 07/07/1901 DEDICATED — Saint Philomena, Chicago
2. 09/08/1901 BLESSED — Our Lady, Help of Christians, Chicago
3. 10/18/1901 DEDICATED — Saint Nicholas, Evanston (German parish)
4. 10/27/1901 DEDICATED — The new Saint Hedwig, Chicago (Polish parish)
5. 06/01/1902 DEDICATED — Saint Mary of the Lake, Chicago
6. 06/08/1902 DEDICATED — Saint Josaphat, Chicago
7. 08/10/1902 DEDICATED — Saint Cyril College for Boys, Chicago

8. 09/06/1902 DEDICATED — Saint Ludmilla, Chicago (Bohemian parish)

9. 11/16/1902 DEDICATED — Saint Benedict, Chicago

10. 11/23/1902 DEDICATED — Saint George, Chicago (Lithuanian parish)

11. 11/30/1902 DEDICATED — Our Lady of Good Counsel, Chicago

12. 06/19/1904 DEDICATED — Saint George, Chicago (Slovenian parish)

13. 06/26/1904 BLESSED—Saint Dominic, Chicago

14. 08/04/1904 DEDICATED — Holy Family, North Chicago

15. 10/16/1904 DEDICATED — Holy Rosary, Chicago (Italian parish)

16. 11/20/1904 DEDICATED — Saint Ambrose, Chicago

17. 06/03/05 DEDICATED — Saint Mary of the Angels, Chicago

18. 06/18/1905 DEDICATED — Saint Francis Xavier, Wilmette

19. 07/02/1905 DEDICATED — Saint Joseph, Libertyville

20. 10/01/1905 DEDICATED — Saint Michael, Chicago (Lithuanian parish)

21. 12/16/1905 DEDICATED — Saint David, Chicago

22. 04/22/1906 DEDICATED — Saint Rita College, Chicago

Additional Occasions Presided over by Auxiliary Bishop Peter J. Muldoon

10/08/1892	Celebrated the first Mass and preached at Our Lady of Lourdes
05/16/1894	Blessed the rebuilt Immaculate Conception Church, Polish parish in Chicago
06/23/1895	Reopened Saint Hedwig's Church, Chicago: previously shuttered after rebellion of Polish parishioners
06/12/1902	Formed Holy Family, North Chicago
09/07/1902	Laid the cornerstone for Saint Boniface, Chicago
06/30/1905	Purchased the Trinity Lutheran Church for Santa Maria Addolorata, Chicago
08/26/1906	Laid the cornerstone for Saint John Berchmans, Chicago
02/03/1907	Celebrated the 25th Anniversary Mass for Assumption of the Blessed Virgin Mary, Italian parish in Chicago
04/04/1907	Dedicated the Oak Park Hospital, Oak Park

A CHRONOLOGY
From the Origins of Chi-ca-gou to the Demolition of Saint Charles Borromeo Parish

THE RAPID GROWTH OF THE Archdiocese of Chicago is tied to the astounding growth of the city. No other city in the entire Midwest traces its historical and religious origins farther back than Chicago.

1673 Chi-ca-gou is a vast, uncharted territory, considered holy ground by local tribes that occupied the region since 6000 B. C.

1673 MAY French explorers Father Jacques Marquette and Louis Jolliet open the limitless wilderness to Western civilization.

1673 JUNE 16 Marquette is the first European to set foot in the land we now know as Illinois.

1673 SEPTEMBER Marquette and Jolliet's portage from the Mississippi River to the Chicago River lead them to the future site of Chicago.

1674 Marquette writes his autobiographical missionary journals, the first documents written in Chicago.

1674–75 Marquette spends a historic and bitter winter on the high grounds of the Onion (Chicago) River (near Damen Avenue).

1675 MAY 18 Marquette dies in Ludington, Michigan.

1675–1775 The area of Chicago remains virtually uninhabited for 100 years.

1784 Chicago becomes an isolated trading post with a Haitian trader, John Baptiste Pointe du Sable, as its first "official" settler.

1795 AUGUST 3 The Treaty of Greenville, Ohio: After the Battle of Fallen Timbers, the Potawatomi and smaller tribes who occupied the territory cede six and a half square miles at the mouth of the Chicago River to General "Mad" Anthony Wayne, giving Americans complete control of the Northwest Territory.

1803–12 Fort Dearborn is erected and named after the secretary of war, Henry Dearborn. The city of Chicago would later build on the site of the Onion River and the Lake of the Illinois (Lake Michigan).

1810 The population of Chicago is approximately 100. Tribal peoples use the land around Chicago as a camping ground for hunting and fishing during warmer seasons.

1812 AUGUST 15 Hostile Potawatomi attack settlers evacuating Fort Dearborn in what's come to be known as the Fort Dearborn Massacre.

1816 A second fort is constructed; it is evacuated in 1837, never to be used again.

1833 The frontier village of Chicago is organized, with John H. Kinzie as its first permanent settler.

1834 Father John Mary Iraneus of Saint Cyr becomes pastor of Saint Mary's—the first church in Chicago. John H. Kinzie becomes the first president of the village of Chicago.

1835 Holy Family parish is formed on the Near West Side at 12th Street and Blue Island Avenue, with Arnold Damen, S.J., as first pastor.

1837 Chicago (with a population of 4,170) is incorporated as a city, with William D. Ogden as its first mayor.

1844 MAY 14 The Diocese of Chicago is formed, with the Right Reverend William D. Quarter as founder. It originally embraced the entire state of Illinois.

1845 The Catholic population of Chicago is 50,000.

1848 The Right Reverend James O. Van de Velde, S.J., becomes Chicago's second bishop.

1850 Waves of German, Irish, and Polish Catholic immigrants begin impacting the expansion of the city.

1851 Chicago becomes the largest corn and wheat market in the country.

1853 The Right Reverend Anthony O'Regan succeeds Van de Velde as bishop.

1854 Chicago becomes the railroad center of the West, with a population of 60,000 and still growing.

1854 SEPTEMBER 30 Calvary is purchased as the first diocesan cemetery. Chicago's bishops were interred there until 1912.

1856 The Chicago Historical Society is formed.

1857 The original site of Fort Dearborn is razed.

1858 Chicago becomes the chief grain supplier of the United States.

1859 The Right Reverend James Duggan succeeds O'Regan as bishop.

1861 APRIL 12 Civil War breaks out between the North and the South. Chicago's population is 110,000, half being foreign born.

1861 NOVEMBER 29 Jeremiah J. Crowley is born in Ireland.

1862 OCTOBER 10 Peter J. Muldoon is born of Irish immigrant parents in California.

1863 Chicago replaces Cincinnati as the pork packing center of the United States.

1864 Chicagoan George F. Root, composer of Civil War ballads, writes "The Battle Cry of Freedom."

1868 Saint Stanislaus Kostka becomes Chicago's first and largest Polish Church.

1870 The Right Reverend Thomas Foley succeeds Duggan as bishop.

1871 OCTOBER 8–10 The Great Chicago Fire burns out an area of four square miles, including more than 20 of the Church's ecclesiastical structures.

1877 Muldoon leaves for four years of college at Saint Mary's in Kentucky, followed by five years of preparation at Saint Mary's Seminary in Baltimore, Maryland.

1880 Archdiocese of Chicago is formed with Patrick A. Feehan as the first archbishop. Some 300,000 people live within city limits of six miles long and three miles wide. Chicago becomes the country's greatest interior city, surpassing Saint Louis, Missouri.

1885 AUGUST Saint Charles Borromeo parish is established for English-speaking persons, from territory previously under the jurisdiction of Saint Jarlath (1869) and Saint Pius V (1874) parishes. Holy Trinity for Germans is established within Saint Charles, the territorial parish, at Taylor and Wolcott (formerly Lincoln Street).

1885 DECEMBER Father Patrick D. Gill is appointed first pastor of Saint Charles and builds a single-building brick parish complex of church, school, convent, and hall. Within seven years, he constructs the massive fortresslike rectory.

1886 JUNE 15 Crowley is ordained at Saint Patrick's Chapel, County Cork, Ireland.

1886 DECEMBER 18 Muldoon is ordained a priest by Reverend Bishop John Loughlin, first bishop of Brooklyn, New York.

1886 The Reverend Peter J. Muldoon, in his first assignment, is sent to Saint Pius V Parish at Ashland and 19th in Chicago, where he remains for about one and a half years.

1888 Feehan appoints Muldoon his secretary and chancellor, moving him from Saint Pius V to the chancery.

1890 The Catholic population of the city of Chicago is 460,000.

1890s Neapolitans, Sicilians, and Calabrians flow into the city on “Mother” Halsted Street.

1894 In the city, nine of ten police officers and eight of ten firefighters are Irish.

1895 OCTOBER Ordained nine years, Muldoon succeeds Father Gill as pastor of Saint Charles, with the commission of building an outstanding Gothic church at the city limits. Gill is sent to build Our Lady of Mount Carmel Church in Lakeview.

1896 JULY 26 The cornerstone of the new Saint Charles Church is laid on holy ground.

1897 FEBRUARY 28 Father Coughlin, Muldoon's uncle, celebrates the first Mass in the new church.

1897 MAY 16 The new Saint Charles Church, with 4,000 members and 800 students in the grammar school, is dedicated.

1897 Chicago switches to electricity.

1899 Construction of two- and three-floor buildings is begun in Saint Charles parish.

1900 The Catholic population in Chicago is 660,000, with the city population being 1,688,575.

1900 Archbishop Feehan nominates Muldoon as his auxiliary bishop—and the Crowley rebellion begins.

1901 JULY 12 Muldoon receives Vatican approval to be auxiliary bishop of Chicago.

1901 JULY 14 Muldoon is appointed vicar general of the Archdiocese of Chicago.

1901 JULY 25 Under tight guard, Muldoon is consecrated auxiliary bishop in Chicago's Holy Name Cathedral.

1901 OCTOBER Jeremiah Crowley is excommunicated from the Catholic Church by Cardinal Martinelli.

1902 JULY 12 Archbishop Feehan dies at the age of 73.

1903 MARCH 10 Muldoon is appointed vicar general by Feehan's successor, Archbishop James E. Quigley.

1903 SEPTEMBER 16 Saint Charles Parochial School lists 1,200 students.

1908 At the suggestion of Archbishop Quigley, the new Diocese of Rockford is formed with Bishop Muldoon as its founder.

1908 DECEMBER Muldoon bids farewell to Chicago and the archdiocese.

1909 FEBRUARY Reverend Edward J. Fox of Saint Anne in Barrington, Illinois, succeeds Muldoon as pastor of Saint Charles.

1909 Some street names are changed. 12th Street becomes Roosevelt Road and Cypress Street becomes Hoyne Avenue.

1910 Chicago's Catholic population tops 1,150,000, with the city total standing at 2,185,283.

1914 World War I begins.

1915 JULY 10 The Most Reverend James E. Quigley dies. Muldoon is nominated for his see but is bypassed for the Right Reverend George Mundelein.

1916 Saint Charles Church reopens after the fire of October 19, 1914.

1917 Muldoon is appointed bishop of Monterey, Los Angeles, California, but later refuses the appointment.

1922 Rumors surface that Crowley has died in Cook County Hospital.

1923 DECEMBER 7 John A. McCarthy from Saint Elizabeth is appointed pastor of Saint Charles.

1926 Robey Street is renamed Damen Avenue to honor Arnold Damen, first pastor of Holy Family Church and a great educator.

1926 JUNE 28 While in St. Louis, Missouri, for the consecration of the new cathedral, Bishop Muldoon is hospitalized with a burst appendix.

1927 MARCH 27 After a long hospitalization, Muldoon returns to Rockford.

1927 OCTOBER 10 Bedridden until his death, Peter J. Muldoon passes away and is buried in Saint Mary's Cemetery in Rockford.

1931 The Right Reverend Matthew "Fritz" Canning, from Saint Lucy's, becomes pastor of Saint Charles during the "Mob" era.

1941 Canning is transferred to Saint Ferdinand, Chicago.

1942 Reverend John A. McMahon is made pastor of Saint Charles.

1952 McMahon is transferred to Saint Sabina, Chicago.

1952 Father Kane becomes pastor at Saint Charles.

1954 Kane rejects a proposal by Samuel Cardinal Stritch to use Saint Charles as the emerging Medical Center parish, signifying the death of Saint Charles as a viable parish community. The about-to-be-leveled Holy Trinity takes over the role of hospital ministry.

1960 Saint Charles celebrates its 75th anniversary.

1961 OCTOBER Father Kane is transferred to another parish.

1962 January Father Patrick J. Navin, assistant at Saint Bridget's of Chicago, becomes the last pastor of Saint Charles.

1966 Saint Charles grammar school is closed.

1968 FEBRUARY 2 Saint Charles is consolidated with Holy Trinity, where all the Saint Charles records are kept.

1968–69 Saint Charles is vandalized and stripped of its rich appointments.

1969 Eighty-four years after its founding in 1885, the entire St. Charles Borromeo complex is razed.

St. Charles Borromeo, reformer and innovator. (Reprinted from *Silver Jubilee: Saint Charles Borromeo: 1885–1910.*)

Appendix C

The Life of Saint Charles Borromeo

WITH THE FOUNDING OF A NEW parish on the open western plains of Chicago in 1885, Archbishop Patrick A. Feehan chose the name of Saint Charles Borromeo, after a bishop who established schools of Christian education for children and helped establish the Catholic seminary system in Italy in the 1500s. As far as saints go, Saint Charles Borromeo isn't as popular as many others, like Saint Patrick, or as warm as Francis of Assisi, or as winsome as Saint Theresa, the Little Flower. But the name Saint Charles Borromeo had a nice ring to it, eliciting the impression of elegance and nobility. Through my study of his sainthood, I find it very significant that Feehan chose Saint Charles Borromeo as patron of the parish complex that Father Peter J. Muldoon built. Saint Charles Borromeo was a bishop who as an educator, a scholar, and a reformer would not tolerate clerical corruption.

Charles Borromeo was born to riches and nobility. His father was Count Gilberto Borromeo, and his mother was Margaret de' Medici of the celebrated de' Medici family of Milan, Italy. Margaret's brother Angelo de' Medici would eventually become Pope Pius IV. Charles, the second of two sons in a family of six children, was born in the family castle of Arona on Lake Maggiore in northern Italy on October 2, 1538. Charles showed early signs of attraction to clerical life. At the age of 12, he received the tonsure, the cutting of the hair by the bishop introducing the candidate into clerical life and symbolizing to the outside world the candidate's intentions. He was sent to the Benedictine Abbey of Saints Gratian and Felinus at Arona for his education. Coming from a powerful family, the young Charles was given the astounding income of a rich Benedictine monastery, a holding of the de' Medici family. Instead of using the abbey's income to indulge his whims, Charles used it to prepare for his career in the Church, and the rest was given to the poor.

Charles continued his studies at the University of Pavia, concentrating on civil and canon law. In his early days, young Charles exhibited a speech impediment and was regarded as a slow student. By the time he earned his doctorate at the age of 22, both of his parents had died. Around this same time, his uncle had been elected Pope. The new pontiff sent for his nephew to join him, and within a short time, Pope Pius IV had showered Charles with many powers, honors, and offices. In his early twenties, Charles Borromeo became a leading player in the papal court. He was not yet a priest but was administrator of the Papal States, the legate of Bologna, the legate of Romagna and Ancona, the protector of Portugal and the Low Countries, administrator of the Catholic cantons in Switzerland, and the supervisor of the Franciscan and Carmelite Orders. With time, Charles grew into his positions and acquired a reputation for honesty and fairness. He was known as being methodical, efficient, and quick. Nothing sat on his desk.

Pius IV had other plans for his mainstay nephew. In 1563, soon after his election, the Pope, with considerable assistance from Charles, reassembled the Council of Trent, a senate of Catholic bishops called to hinder the Protestant Reformation that was consuming much of Europe. The Council of Trent had been suspended since 1552. While the council was in session, Charles's older brother died, placing the vast family holdings in his hands. But Charles diverted the overwhelming fortune to his uncle. Without yet even being ordained a priest, Charles had already served mightily for the Church. In 1563 he finally became a priest, and two months later he became bishop of Milan, as well as cardinal of priests. That is progress.

After the death of Pius IV, Charles put aside his many chores and returned to Milan, where he reestablished the long-neglected diocese that had not had a resident bishop for 80 years. He worked diligently to elevate the spiritual life of his Catholic people. Charles turned over all of his income and the wealth he had inherited from his family estate to the poor. At night, when he was alone, he removed the opulent bishop's robes for a tattered, worn cassock and spent his time in study and prayer. The cardinal priest lived his private life simply, modestly, and in self-discipline.

During his work for the Church, Charles Borromeo founded the Confraternity of Christian Doctrine, developing the first Sunday schools and teaching catechism to children. In addition, while bishop of Milan, Charles founded a society of secular priests in 1578 known as the Society of Saint Ambrose.

In his declining years, Charles opposed and fought off a group of corrupt clergy of his diocese, a decayed penitential order that controlled the income of scores of clerics and monastics attempting to enhance their own good lives. In anger and vengeance, some of them plotted the assassination of Charles, actually firing shots at him while he was at evening prayer. Charles survived the murder attempt, forgave his attackers, and succeeded in the reform of the corrupt community.

Saint Charles spent much of his time in the mountains and hills beyond and north of his diocese, instructing whomever he could—shepherds, laborers, the poor, the disadvantaged, a tapestry of the dispossessed, hungry, and unlettered—in the words of the Gospel. While in the hills, Charles became very ill and returned to Milan. In a short time, he became rapidly worse and died on November 4, 1584, at the relatively young age of 46. After his death, a memorial was erected in Il Duomo, the Cathedral of Milan, where his body is interred. Known for his goodness and holiness, his canonization took place in 1610, just 26 years after his death, a very short time as far as canonization goes.

Upon reflection, Saint Charles Borromeo, one of the towering figures of the Catholic Reformation, seems to have much in common with Bishop Peter J. Muldoon. Both burst onto the Catholic scene at an early age, were dedicated to Catholic education, and had to fend off the attacks of unscrupulous brother priests. It seems as if there just couldn't be a more fitting name for the church that Muldoon built. Today the Catholic Church celebrates the feast day of Saint Charles Borromeo on November 4.

"ON LOVING THE POOR"

—by William A. Schumacher

Father Bill Schumacher's article "On Loving the Poor" first appeared in America, *a Jesuit magazine, on May 28, 1958. For a long time I debated within myself whether to include this entire article at the end of the book. After all, Father Schumacher did play an important part in my life and* Muldoon *is dedicated to him and my wife Della. This article addresses the core of our parish lives. It is about dealing with the poor, one of the problems with Kane and St. Charles Borromeo when I served there.*

ST. VINCENT DEPAUL ONCE SAID: "The poor are our most demanding masters; we must love them so they will forgive us the bread that we gave them." We rarely think of him as a master of paradox, yet in that epigram St. Vincent struck, three centuries ago, a profound truth about Christian charity. It seems strange at first glance to think of the poor as our masters; we tend, rather, to regard them as our inferiors, the recipients of our liberality.

But St. Vincent was looking to the real fruit of Christian charity, the spiritual benefit of the giver. It is axiomatic in theology that pure, disinterested love of God is impossible; the virtue of charity—that is, the love of God for His own sake—will always have overtones of our own spiritual profit from the very act of loving God. This is also true when the same virtue is directed toward its other proper object—namely the children of God, who are to be loved for His sake. When we truly love the poor, we stand to profit thereby. The poor, then, are really our benefactors, our masters, who have the right to demand love in God's name, and who confer on those who love them an eternal benefit.

A VISIT TO THE POOR

However, we cannot love what we do not know. True love is intensely personal; it cannot be accomplished by remote control. We cannot love the poor merely through a check or a gift; we must first come to know them. Come with me into the homes of the poor, here in the affluent United States, 1960. Whatever their race or color; whatever their religion or lack of it; whether they speak broken English, sloppy Spanish, or in the heavily accented tones of the Southern hills and fields—all the poor are very much alike. Climb the steps to the third-floor rear of a tenement, making your way past abandoned baby buggies, old tire casings and discarded clothing. Be careful to step over gaps where boards are missing from the stairs. (When there are no locks on the doors, removing a few planks from the back steps makes an effective barrier against surreptitious entry into a third-floor flat.) Don't forget to look for the poor living in so-called cottages, shacks located on the backs of lots which seem to be occupied completely by small factories and filling stations. You will find the poor there, too, down that littered path and behind that broken fence—living where you would never expect to find anyone at all.

Wherever they live, you will find the poor enveloped in an all-embracing odor, with mingled scents of un-washed bodies, moldy clothes, strong cooking smells, escaping gas and, in winter, the piercing reek of fuel from the stoves. The buildings in which the poor lived were erected some fifty to eighty years ago; time and neglect have taken their toll in broken doorjambs, sagging floors, peeling walls, leaky pipes and balky plumbing. Be sure to bring a flashlight if you make this trip at night; it will spare you many a bad fall and embarrassing situation.

Beyond where the poor live, we must meet them face to face. From a natural viewpoint they are not a very attractive people. Defeated by life, old before their time, they seem suspicious at first acquaintance. When you come to know them better, you will learn that this is a deep-seated shrewdness born of years of experience in detecting phonies and frauds. Surrounded by crudity, living in the midst of every sort of degradation, accustomed to disease and corruption, grown used to all varieties of sin from childhood, these people cannot be fooled or tricked. All the effects of original sin are well known to the poor; the weaknesses and shortcomings of human nature are drilled into them every day of their lives. Hammer blows of human cruelty and selfishness have fallen on their hearts, uncushioned by the conventions that protect the rest of us. What wonder, then, that something twisted and misshapen has occasionally resulted.

These, then, are the poor who are our most demanding masters; these are the people we must love if we are to love God. But what is lovable about them? Only the image of God in their souls is an adequate object of true charity. The whole problem lies in seeing this image in such a place. Philosophy tells us that God is Goodness, Truth and Beauty. His image is hard to find in those whose lives are choked with evil, lies and ugliness. Only the virtue of faith, the acceptance of God's word that these are, indeed, His beloved children and the brothers of His Son—only such faith makes this kind of love possible. In the world's eyes they are worthless, yet the price which God paid for each one of them is the death of His own Son on the cross. Only the crucifix is the right price tag for each of the souls of the poor.

But once we have come to know the poor, then we must learn to love them. More than this, we must learn to love them in such a way that the expression of our love will not corrupt its spiritual fruits and make a hollow mockery of the love itself.

We cannot truly love the poor with "charity": in the do-gooder, Lady Bountiful sense, because this sort of charity is often only a thinly disguised selfishness. Those "charitable" Catholics whose acts of love consist of graciously bestowing a gift on some waif with a photographer in attendance remind me always of Christ's story of the Pharisee, who gave his alms to the accompaniment of blaring trumpets in the streets of Jerusalem or by the picture on the society page; there is no spiritual reward to be gained. What could have been profitable for eternal life has been wasted in attempting to buy the fickle praise of men.

This love of God in His own poor will never be carried out in practice merely by writing a check, even for those women we have come to know. What young lady would take a lover seriously who made his proposal by mail, money order enclosed? If we claim to love the poor, it must be with qualities of a lover—a burning personal interest in their happiness both here and hereafter, a concern for their welfare in every sense, a compassion for their weaknesses, an understanding of their all too human frailties.

It would be easy to love the poor if they would respond in kind; it is very difficult to offer love to those who take it for granted and spit in your eye. Yet only this kind of love is worthy to be called by the noble name of Christian charity since Christ our Lord loved us in this way. As St. Paul reminds us: "It is hard enough to find anyone who will die on behalf of a just man, although perhaps there may be those who will face death for one deserving. But here, as if God meant to prove how well He loves us, it was while we were still sinners, that Christ, in His own appointed time, died for us." (Romans 5:8–9)

The poor are shrewd and all our protestations of interest and concern, all our well-meaning compassion and understanding will be rejected as a sham and a fraud unless it is backed up by self sacrifice. This is the ultimate test of love, the willingness to put oneself out—in time, in convenience, in cold cash until it hurts. The poor are realists; they know from bitter experience that pious words do not put food in children's mouths, nor do beautiful sentiments put shoes on their feet.

But if merely writing a check is not enough to love the poor, how then are we to do it? Did you ever think of learning about a poor family, literally feeding and clothing them? An experience of this sort can teach us more about poverty and its effects than all the sociology texts ever written. It can also be quite humbling and thought provoking.

WHEN LOVE IS PRACTICAL

Could you pick up a poor expectant mother and drive her to a prenatal clinic, saving her a long walk in the cold? Could you visit some of the most pathetic poor people of all, the old ones whose lives are leaking away in a dark, forgotten room, surrounded by the pitiful relics of a lifetime of suffering? Could you stomach a trip to the county hospital, to an old people's home, to a Catholic hospital for unmarried mothers—not just a visit, a tour of inspection, but hours of heart-rending suffering perhaps, just sitting there and listening to the sick pour out the tragedy of their lives? Would you have the love and patience necessary to teach catechism to a child not quite yet mentally deficient to be placed in an institution? No one who has never tried these works of mercy can know what bittersweet experiences they can be, how our very understandable natural loathing can be turned into a spiritual joy by the alchemy of God's grace.

Loving the poor is not something optional for a Christian; it is the very essence of his faith, and it makes sense only in the light of the faith. It is easy to love lepers in Asia, when someone else changes their bandages; it is easy to love orphans in our own city, when devoted Sisters care for them day and night. But it is repulsive, it is awkward, it is sometimes embarrassing, it can make us uncomfortable to think about really and truly loving the poor in person.

When the followers of John came to Christ to ask if He were the Messiah, our Lord made the preaching of the Gospel to the poor the sure sign of His office as Savior. Love of the poor has always remained the certain mark of His true followers, of His real lovers. And His beloved apostle, St. John remarks: "Yes, we must love God; He gave us His love first. If a man boasts of loving God, while he hates his own brother, and has no love for him; he is a liar. He has seen his brother, and has no love for him, what love can he have for the God he has never seen? No, this is the divine command that has been given us; the man who loves God must be the one who loves his brother as well." (John 4:20–21)

Christ Himself has given us a very practical reason for this personal love of the poor. On the most momentous day of our lives, He will say to the elect: "I was hungry and you gave me food, thirsty, and you gave me drink; I was a stranger and you brought me home, naked, and you clothed me, sick, and you cared for me, a prisoner and you came to see me. . . . Believe me, when you did it for one of my brethren, you did it to Me." And others will hear, to their eternal sorrow, that the contrary of this is also true . . . "When you refused it to one of the least of my brethren, you refused it to Me." (Matthew 25: 35–46)

FR. SCHUMACHER, a priest serving the parish of St. Charles Borromeo, Chicago, here sends us his first venture into the field of writing.

Bibliography

BOOKS

American National Bibliography. New York: Oxford Press, 1909.

Bielski, Ursula. *Chicago Haunts.* Chicago: Lake Claremont Press, 1998.

Boros, Ladislaus. *The Mystery of Death.* New York: Herder & Herder, 1965.

Brown, Thomas N. *Irish-American Nationalism,* 1870–1890. Philadelphia: J.P. Lippincott, 1966.

Caritas Christi: Urget Nos. *A History of the Offices, Agencies, and Institutions of the Archdiocese of Chicago.* Vol. I. Chicago: New World Publishing Company, 1981.

A Catholic Commentary on Holy Scriptures. New York: Thomas Nelson & Sons, 1954.

Collier's Encyclopedia. New York: P.F. Collier Inc., 1996.

Crowley, Patrick J. *A Rebel of Many Causes.* N.p., n.d.

Decet Meminisse Fratrum: A Necrology of the Diocesan Priests of the Chicago Archdiocese, 1837–1959. Chicago: Archdiocese of Chicago, n.d.

Encyclopedia Americana, International Edition. Danbury, CT: Grolier Inc., 2000.

Garragan, Gilbert J. *The Catholic Church in Chicago, 1673–1871.* Chicago: Loyola University Press, 1921.

Havighurst, Walter. *Heartland: Ohio, Indiana, Illinois.* New York: Harper & Row Publishers, 1956.

Higgins, John F. *Necrology of Chicago Diocesan Priests.* Chicago: Ptg Co., 1937.

Hoffer, William. *Saved!* (*The Andrea Doria*). New York: Simon & Schuster, 1979.

Illustrated Souvenir of the Archdiocese of Chicago. Chicago: R.H. Fleming Publishing Co., 1916.

The Jerusalem Bible. Garden City, NY: Doubleday & Company, 1966.

Koenig, Harry C. *A History of the Parishes of the Archdiocese of Chicago.* Vols. I and II. Chicago: Archdiocese of Chicago, 1980.

Lind, Alan R. *Chicago Surface Lines: An Illustrated History.* Park Forest, IL: Transport History Press, 1979.

McCaffrey, Lawrence J., Ellen Skerrit, Michael F. Funchion, and Charles Fanning. *The Irish in Chicago.* Chicago: University of Illinois Press, 1987.

McCain, W. Ross. *Chicago City Directory—1844.* Chicago: Cook County Department, 1844.

Miller, Robert R. *That All May Be One: A History of the Rockford Diocese.* Rockford, IL: Diocese of Rockford, 1976.

Nevins, Albert J. *Our American Catholic Heritage.* Huntington, IN: Our Sunday Visitor, Inc., 1972.

The New Catholic Encyclopedia. Palatine: Jack Heraty & Associates, Inc., 1972.

The New Encyclopædia Britannica, 2002. Chicago: Encyclopædia Britannica, Inc., 2002.

100 Years—The History of the Church of the Holy Name, 1874–1974. Chicago: n.p., 1949.

Prince Michael of Greece. *Living with Ghosts.* New York: W.W.J. Norton & Company, 1955.

Roeper, Richard. *Urban Legends.* Franklin Lakes, NJ: Career Press, 1999.

Schumacher, Reverend William A. "On Loving the Poor," *America.* May 28, 1958.

Shanabruch, Charles. *Chicago's Catholics.* Notre Dame, IN: University of Notre Dame Press, 1981.

Silver Jubilee: Saint Charles Borromeo: 1885–1910. Chicago: Press of the Mayer and Millen Company, 1910.

Souvenir of the Archdiocese of Chicago, *Commemorating the Installation of the Most Reverend George W. Mundelein, D.D. February 19, 1916.* Chicago: Archdiocese of Chicago, 1916.

Trevelyan, G.M. *Garibaldi & the Thousand.* New York: Thomas Nelson & Sons, 1860.

Vann, Joseph. *Lives of the Saints.* New York: John J. Crowley & Co., 1954.

Wibbelt, Augustin. *The Blessed Peace of Death.* New York: Joseph F. Wagner, Inc., 1966.

Winslow, Charles S. *Indians of the Chicago Region.* Chicago: Superland Printing Services, 1946.

NEWSPAPERS

Chicago Catholic New World

Chicago Daily News

Chicago Daily Tribune

Chicago Defender

Chicago Herald

New York Times

Author Acknowledgments

Dan Facchini, my indispensable collaborator, editor, and wordsmith.

David Facchini, the family artist, sensitive to transforming the text into vivid illustrations.

James E. Wilbur, editor and proofreader without peer; invaluable adviser on this book's historical, liturgical, and theological accuracy.

Marko Kevo, who worked with David in taking contemporary photographs.

Dolores Madlener, "Church Clips," *The Catholic New World.*

Tim Unsworth of *National Catholic Reporter.*

Sharon Woodhouse of Lake Claremont Press.

The Most Reverend Raymond E. Goedert, Sister Bride Hanley, B.V.M., the Reverends Daniel J. Collins, John Dolciamore, Andrew J. Greeley, Willard F. Jabusch, John Lynch, Edward J. Norkett, Thomas V. Millea, James F. Morriarty, Patrick O'Malley, and Robert C. Rizzo, and most profoundly, Reverend Thomas Sularz.

The late Reverends William A. Schumacher, Andrew J. McDonough, and Raynor E. Richter.

Julie A. Stazik, archdiocesan research archivist of the Cardinal Bernardin Center; Reverend Kenneth O'Malley, C.P., librarian of the Catholic Theological Union; the Chicago Historical Society, the Newberry Library, and the Mayfair, Conrad Sulzer Regional, and Harold Washington Main public libraries of Chicago.

For typing my manuscript: Theresa and Richard Carsello, Patricia Carsello, Della Facchini, Jodi Facchini, Maureen Hillebrand, and most especially, Jennifer Slusher.

Len Cicero, Dino Marchiori, Mike Owens, Greg Scherrer, and Erik Varela.

The late Paul E. Flaherty, dear friend and attorney at law who started me on this project.

Early mainstay supporters: Mercedes Gilpatric, Bill and Lucille Riordan, and Fred and Anne Schwartz.

Catherine McGivney of Connelly Roberts & McGivney LLC and Gerard Facchini, attorneys at law.

Readers of my early text: Phil and Jean Addante, Harry and Pat Benjamin, Jack and Adela Greeley, Marty and Carole Hegarty, Karen Koegler, Pat McParland, Ivette Paredes, John Pemberton, David and Sherri Pemberton, Barry and Donna Rankin, and Jim and Joan Wilbur.

The Romeos: Dom Cronin, Pete Dunne, Ed Fitzharris, John Giannini, Ed Gilpatric, Marty Hegarty, George Helfrich, John Lynch, Jerry Maloney, Bob McClory, Bill McGlynn, Frank McGrath, Fran Moroney, Roger O'Brien, Barry Rankin, Tim Unsworth, and Jim Wilbur.

Gulliver's Restaurant proprietors Jerry and Nancy Widmer Freeman.

Doctors Michael J. Plunkett, James V. Yeung, and Sum Sup Kim and the staff of Swedish Covenant Hospital and the Galter Life Center Cardiac Rehabilitation Program, Chicago.

Nancy Forrester, Barbara Wagner, and the staff of Niles Neomedica Dialysis Center on Milwaukee Avenue, Niles, Illinois.

The Rogues of '56

Index

Italicized page numbers indicate photos.

E

F

G

H

I

J

K

N

O

P

Q

T

U

V

W

Dan, Rocco, and David Facchini (left to right). (Photo by David Facchini.)

About the Authors

A FIRST-TIME AUTHOR IN HIS early seventies, **Rocco Facchini** is a native Chicagoan, born to Italian immigrant parents, Gerardo and Maria. Poised for the religious life at an early age, Rocco attended Our Lady of the Angels school, Quigley Preparatory Seminary, and St. Mary of the Lake Seminary. Rocco was ordained on May 1, 1956, and served as a Chicago Diocesan priest for 15 years at St. Charles Borromeo, St. John Bosco, and Our Lady, Help of Christians parishes, before resigning from the priesthood in March 1971.

As a layperson, Rocco first worked as a real estate broker and then as a Certified Property Manager for Wirtz Realty Corporation for 27 years. He married Della on July 4, 1972, and has two children, Daniel and David, who both collaborated with him on this book. Rocco continues to live in Chicago and has the distinction of being a Papal Knight of the Holy Sepulchre. Since his retirement in 1999, he has begun writing about life as a priest, life as a dialysis patient, and the many eventful things and interesting people in his life.

Rocco's older son, **Dan Facchini**, has Bachelor's Degrees in Economics and English from Northern Illinois University and a Master's Degree in Public Service Management from DePaul University. Dan married Jodi in 2001. When not writing, he works as Development Director for Housing Opportunities and Maintenance for the Elderly (H.O.M.E.), is Chapter Advisor for Pi Kappa Alpha Fraternity at Northern Illinois University, and plays rugby for the Chicago Griffins Rugby Club.

A graduate of Columbia College Chicago with a Bachelor's Degree in Film and Animation, **David Facchini** is an artist living in Chicago. He juggles freelance animation, film, video, photography, illustration, set design, sculpting, screenwriting, acting, and improvisational theater. He has recently completed a short stop-motion animated film several years in the making, *Vodka Monster*, to be released in festivals in the summer of 2003.

OTHER BOOKS FROM LAKE CLAREMONT PRESS

GHOSTS AND GRAVEYARDS

Chicago Haunts: Ghostlore of the Windy City

More Chicago Haunts: Scenes from Myth and Memory

Graveyards of Chicago: The People, History, Art, and Lore of Cook County Cemeteries

Haunted Michigan: Recent Encounters with Active Spirits

More Haunted Michigan: New Encounters with Ghosts of the Great Lakes State

CHICAGO HISTORY

Chicago's Midway Airport: The First Seventy-Five Years

The Chicago River: A Natural and Unnatural History

Great Chicago Fires: Historic Blazes That Shaped a City

Near West Side Stories: Struggles for Community in Chicago's Maxwell Street Neighborhood

The Golden Age of Chicago Children's Television

CHICAGO SPECIALTY GUIDEBOOKS

The Hoofs & Guns of the Storm: Chicago's Civil War Connections

A Cook's Guide to Chicago

Literary Chicago: A Book Lover's Tour of the Windy City

Hollywood on Lake Michigan: 100 Years of Chicago and the Movies

The Streets & San Man's Guide to Chicago Eats

MIDWEST TRAVEL

Ticket to Everywhere: The Best of Detours Travel Column

A Native's Guide to Chicago, 4th Ed.

A Native's Guide to Northwest Indiana

CHILDREN AND FAMILIES

Creepy Chicago

The Firefighter's Best Friend: Lives and Legends of Chicago Firehouse Dogs

Chicago Haunts: Ghostlore of the Windy City
by Ursula Bielski
From ruthless gangsters to restless mail order kings, from the Fort Dearborn Massacre to the St. Valentine's Day Massacre, the phantom remains of the passionate people and volatile events of Chicago history have made the Second City second to none in the annals of American ghostlore. Bielski captures over 160 years of this haunted history with her distinctive blend of lively storytelling, in-depth historical research, exclusive interviews, and insights from parapsychology. Called "a masterpiece of the genre," "a must-read," and "an absolutely first-rate-book" by reviewers, *Chicago Haunts* continues to earn the praise of critics and readers alike.
0-9642426-7-2, October 1998, softcover, 277 pages, 29 photos, $15

More Chicago Haunts: Scenes from Myth and Memory
by Ursula Bielski
50 new stories! Step back inside "the biggest ghost town in America."
1-893121-04-6, October 2000, softcover, 312 pages, 50 photos, $15

Graveyards of Chicago: The People, History, Art, and Lore of Cook County Cemeteries
by Matt Hucke and Ursula Bielski
Like the livelier neighborhoods that surround them, Chicago's cemeteries are often crowded, sometimes weary, ever-sophisticated, and full of secrets. They are home not only to thousands of individuals who fashioned the city's singular culture and character, but also to impressive displays of art and architecture, landscaping and limestone, egoism and ethnic pride, and the constant reminder that although physical life must end for us all, personal note—and notoriety—last forever.
0-9642426-4-8, November 1999, softcover, 228 pages, 168 photos, $15

Haunted Michigan:
Recent Encounters with Active Spirits
by Rev. Gerald S. Hunter
Within these pages you will not find ancient ghost stories or legendary accounts of spooky events of long ago. Instead, Rev. Hunter shares his investigations into modern ghost stories—active hauntings that continue to this day. Wherever you may dwell, these tales of Michigan's ethereal residents are sure to make you think about

the possibility, as Hunter suggests, that we are not always alone within the confines of our happy homes.
1-893121-10-0, October 2000, softcover, 207 pages, 20 photos, $12.95

More Haunted Michigan:
New Encounters with Ghosts of the Great Lakes State
by Rev. Gerald S. Hunter
Rev. Hunter invited readers of *Haunted Michigan* to open their minds to the presence of the paranormal all around them. They opened their minds . . . and unlocked a grand repository of their own personal supernatural experiences. Hunter investigated these modern, active hauntings and recounts the most chilling and most unusual here for you, in further confirmation that the Great Lakes State may be one of the most haunted places in the country.
1-893121-29-1, February 2003, softcover, 260 pages, 22 photos, $15

Creepy Chicago: A Ghosthunter's Tales of the City's Scariest Sites
by Ursula Bielski
Nineteen true tales of Chicago's famous phantoms, haunted history, and unsolved mysteries, for readers ages 8-12.
1-893121-15-1, August 2003, softcover, illustrations, glossary, bibliography, $8

REGIONAL HISTORY

Chicago's Midway Airport: The First Seventy-Five Years
By Christopher Lynch
Midway was Chicago's first official airport, and for decades it was the busiest airport in the nation, and then the world. Lynch captures the spirit of adventure of the dawn of flight, combining narrative, essays, and oral histories to tell the engrossing tale of Midway Airport and the evolution of aviation right along with it. Recommended by the *Chicago Sun-Times.*
1-893121-18-6, January 2003, softcover, 10" x 8", 201 pages, 205 historic and contemporary photos, $19.95

Great Chicago Fires: Historic Blazes That Shaped a City
by David Cowan
As Chicago changed from agrarian outpost to industrial giant, it would be visited time and again by some of the worst infernos in American history—fires that sparked not only banner headlines but, more importantly, critical upgrades in fire safety laws across the globe. Acclaimed author and veteran firefighter David Cowan tells the story of the other "great" Chicago fires, noting the causes, consequences, and historical context of each. In transporting

readers beyond the fireline and into the ruins, Cowan brings readers up close to the heroism, awe, and devastation generated by the fires that shaped Chicago.
1-893121-07-0, August 2001, softcover, 10" x 8", 167 pages, 86 historic and contemporary photographs, $19.95

CHICAGO SPECIALTY GUIDEBOOKS

Hollywood on Lake Michigan: 100 Years of Chicago and the Movies

by Arnie Bernstein, foreword by *Soul Food* director George Tillman, Jr.
This engaging history and street guide finally gives Chicago and Chicagoans due credit for their prominent role in moviemaking history, from the silent era to the present. With trivia, special articles, historic and contemporary photos, film profiles, anecdotes, and exclusive interviews with dozens of personalities, including Studs Terkel, Roger Ebert, Gene Siskel, Dennis Franz, Harold Ramis, Joe Mantegna, Bill Kurtis, Irma Hall, and Tim Kazurinsky. Winner of an American Regional History Publishing Award: 1st Place—Midwest!
0-9642426-2-1, December 1998, softcover, 364 pages, 80 photos, $15

MIDWEST TRAVEL

A Native's Guide to Chicago, 4th Edition

by Lake Claremont Press
Venture into the nooks and crannies of everyday Chicago with this comprehensive budget guide that picks up where other guidebooks leave off. Over 400 pages of free, inexpensive, and unusual things to do in the Windy City make this the perfect resource for tourists, business travelers, visiting suburbanites, and resident Chicagoans. Called the "best guidebook for locals" in *New City*'s 1999 "Best of Chicago" issue!
1-893121-23-2, September 2003, softcover, 450 pages, photos, maps, $15.95

A Native's Guide to Northwest Indiana

by Mark Skertic
At the southern tip of Lake Michigan, in the crook between Chicagoland and southwestern Michigan, lies Northwest Indiana, a region of natural diversity, colorful history, abundant recreational opportunities, small town activities, and urban diversions. Whether you're a life-long resident, new in the area, or just passing through, let native Mark Skertic be your personal tour guide of the best the region has to offer.
1-893121-08-9, August 2003, softcover, photos, maps, $15.00

ORDER FORM

Title	Qty	Price	Total
Muldoon: A True Chicago Ghost Story	______	@ $15.00 =	________
Chicago Haunts	______	@ $15.00 =	________
More Chicago Haunts	______	@ $15.00 =	________
Graveyards of Chicago	______	@ $15.00 =	________
Haunted Michigan	______	@ $12.95 =	________
More Haunted Michigan	______	@ $15.00 =	________
Creepy Chicago	______	@ $8.00 =	________
Great Chicago Fires	______	@ $19.95 =	________
Chicago's Midway Airport	______	@ $19.95 =	________
Hollywood on Lake Michigan	______	@ $15.00 =	________
________________	______	@ $____ =	________

Subtotal: ________
Less Discount: ________
New Subtotal: ________
8.75% Sales Tax for Illinois Residents: ________
Shipping: ________
TOTAL: ________

Name____
Address____
City____________________________ **State**__________ **Zip**__________
Please enclose check, money order, or credit card information.
Visa/Mastercard#______________________________ **Exp.** ____
Signature____

Discounts when you order multiple copies!
2 books—10% off total, 3–4 books—20% off,
5–9 books—25% off, 10+ books—40% off

—Low shipping fees—
$2.50 for the first book and $.50 for each additional book,
with a maximum charge of $8.

Order by mail, phone, fax, or e-mail.

4650 N. Rockwell St.
Chicago, IL 60625
773/583-7800
773/583-7877 (fax)
lcp@lakeclaremont.com
www.lakeclaremont.com